Herding Chickens

Innovative Techniques for
Project Management

GREG & DIANE,

GOOD LUCK ON ALL

YOUR PROJECTS.

Dan

Herding Chickens

Innovative Techniques for Project Management

Dan Bradbary and

David Garrett

San Francisco   London

Publisher: Neil Edde
Acquisitions and Developmental Editor: Heather O'Connor
Production Editor: Leslie E.H. Light
Technical Editor: Patti Jensen
Copyeditor: Sarah H. Lemaire
Compositor: Maureen Forys, Happenstance Type-O-Rama
Graphic Illustrator: Jeffery Wilson, Happenstance Type-O-Rama
Proofreaders: Nancy Riddiough, Jim Brook
Indexer: Nancy Guenther
Book Designer: Maureen Forys, Happenstance Type-O-Rama
Cover Designer: Caryl Gorska, Gorska Design
Cover Illustrator/Photographer: Debra McClinton

Library of Congress Card Number: 2004113399

ISBN: 0-7821-4383-0

To our valued readers,

Harbor Light Press was created as an imprint of Sybex, Inc. to help business professionals acquire the practical skills and knowledge they need to meet today's most pressing business challenges.

Our books serve the people responsible for getting the job done—project managers charged with delivering a product on time and under budget; human resource directors faced with a complex array of resource decisions; support staff determined to exceed the goals set for them; and others who recognize that great business plans are only as good as the people who implement and manage them.

Harbor Light Press is committed to publishing authoritative, reliable, yet engaging business books written by authors who are outstanding instructors and experienced business professionals. The goal for all of our books is to connect with our readers, to understand their needs, and to provide them with solutions that they can put to use immediately.

Neil Edde
Publisher
Harbor Light Press

We'd like to offer this to all of you who became project managers whether you meant to or not. Do you remember the day when your boss said, "I've got a little project for you?" At precisely that moment, you became a member of the world's largest accidental profession.

Acknowledgments

Nothing's as bad as page of acknowledgments that runs on forever, thanking everyone from mom to Great Aunt Tilly and her dog, Squat. So in the interest of brevity, we'd each like to thank the other for his hard work, and, of course, we'd like to thank the gifted staff at Sybex for not slapping us silly at any point in the writing of this book.

Contents

Introduction

Squawk

Question: Are your feathers ruffled?

Does the notion of running projects in your company, school, not-for-profit, or other place of business leave you weak in the knees? Does it trouble you? Are you the least bit confused about how to get things done, on time and on budget? If you are, don't get flustered. This is the book for you.

Is your project team as functional as a family you'd find on Dr. Phil? Do you have projects that are frayed at the seams or, even worse, unraveling from the inside out? Do you have projects that are half-done, undone, or about to lay an egg? Don't be ashamed: Most of us do. It's just the way of the world, a simple law of the universe. And if you're among those managers with projects that aren't quite going as planned, then we've got one hell of a book for you.

Herding Chickens

Welcome to the fine art of herding chickens, the art of mastering project management in, shall we say, unconventional ways. It's the art of running projects from start to finish with nary a hiccup, and herding your team— your lawyers, doctors, engineers, computer hackers, planners, doers, thinkers, dreamers, presidents and vice-presidents, CEOs and CIOs, and fellow project managers—in the right direction at the right time.

(A brief diversion: You may have heard the term *herding cats* before, since cats are roughly as easy to herd as Komodo dragons. And indeed, for a time we thought of calling the book *Herding Cats*, to express how tough it is to get the many people on your team to move in the same direction at once, and to get things done with little fuss and fury. But cats, no matter how they refuse our attempts to herd them, always move with grace and dignity. They slink about the ground like they own it, and if perchance they should fall, they always land on their feet. Not so with your team and its members. In today's office, we fly around like chickens with our heads lopped off, and if something goes wrong—and something always goes wrong—then one of us (most often you, the project manager) will see his head on the chopping block. Thus *Herding Chickens* is an apt metaphor for the nearly impossible job of today's project manager and chicken-in-chief.)

Herding Chickens is all about project management, but not the kind of project management you're used to. If you're already a project manager and you've received your PMP, you're used to reading information like this:

> *Among the central process groups, the links are iterated—planning provides executing with a document project plan early on, and then provides documented updates to the plan as the project progresses....*
> *In addition, the project management process groups are not discrete, one-time events; they are overlapping activities that occur at varying levels of intensity through each phase of the project.*

Yikes. That's an excerpt from the famous PMBOK, *The Project Management Body of Knowledge* published by the Project Management Institute (www.pmi.org). And indeed, if you've got the slightest interest in project management at all, that's the place to go. The PMBOK is *the* authority on the field and an essential stopping place on the route to project management mastery.

But as fond as we are of the PMBOK, and as much as we believe in its value, *Herding Chickens* is different. It's a fun, funny, often irreverent look at some of the least-used (but most useful) notions in running projects. It's an oddball collection of tips and tricks for PMs, managers, and plain old workers who are willing to bend the rules to get things done. And we think it's highly effective.

Glad To Meet Ya

Who is *we*? *We* is Dan Bradbary, a project manager with a resume 30 years in the making. As founder and owner of Project Management Services, Inc.—one of the nation's largest PM firms—he's worked for much of the Fortune 1000, and the budgets of his projects total more than five billion dollars. His expertise runs the gamut from biotech to healthcare, mergers and acquisitions, telecom, IT, and finance. He's also an MBA, a Registered Professional Engineer, and a Southern gentleman with a taste for yachting and long, winding runs on the beach.

We is also David Garrett, who last took a long, winding run on the beach when Carter was in office. (Dave thinks the right approach to exercise is to lie down until the urge to do it goes away.) Note: Dave is not a PM. He's a self-avowed egghead who plays with technology like kids play with toys, and an expert at using the Web, database systems, and all kinds of gadgets to improve corporate efficiency. As well he should be: In the eight years since he left college he's worked for everyone from mom-and-pop shops to the Fortune 100, building everything from websites to intranet to extranets with some of the best PMs in the business. And along the way, he's written a couple of hundred articles on business technology.

Together, Dan and Dave have developed a unique and (some would say) iconoclastic way of getting things done in the corporate space. Dan has decades of project management tricks up his sleeve, most of which he learned the hard way—by doing. That's what happens when you're asked to re-tool the network of a major airline on a budget that's less than half of what you need, or to oversee a dozen projects in a startup where Nobel laureates, Ph.D.s, and world-class researchers are as common as secretaries. Dave, on the other hand, has used and abused every kind of technology since the wheel, from the smallest PDA to the biggest network, and learned how to wring every last drop of goodness from them for running projects. When you put their two heads together, you get:

- One uber-project manager who's seen it all and has the war stories—and good advice—to prove it

- One uppity technogeek who knows how to merge project management and bleeding-edge technology

- One unique way of running projects as a result

Is This Book For You?

We call it *herding chickens*, a reference to how tough it is to get a project team, so often composed of everyone under the sun from every discipline in the world, to move in the same direction at once. In a nutshell, that's the project manager's job, and good project managers—good chicken herders—know how to do it with flair.

After all, at base, projects are delivered by people. Sure, projects are all about tasks and deadlines and products and schedules and memos and e-mails and all the other things that go into making them. But none of those things exist without *people* to dream them up and make them happen. People are your single most important asset on any project you run, from the smallest to the largest, and knowing how to manage them—how to herd them—is the difference between a spectacular project and a total dud.

Of course, you may already be a chicken herder without knowing it. Take this quiz to find out.

1. **When you have project updates or announcements to share with your team, do you**

   A) Type them up on an IBM Selectric, make photocopies, and attach them to carrier pigeons for distribution?

B) Send them out by e-mail?

C) Post them to a project intranet customized for your project team?

2. **When you need to get your team to communicate better, do you**

A) Bribe them with gifts, like free tickets to Uzbekistan?

B) Bring in cutting-edge tools like the Myers-Briggs Type Indicator or the MTR-i?

C) Have (yet another) meeting to hash it out?

3. **When you're ahead of time and under budget with your project, do you**

A) Sacrifice a goat to thank the gods, after dancing an unseemly dance of joy on the conference room table?

B) Analyze the ripple effects of your schedule, with special care for the time cost of money?

C) Keep pushing to finish early and under budget?

4. **At the start of each project, do you**

A) Perform a SWOT analysis with your team?

B) Leave advanced risk planning to yourself and others trained in the field?

C) Give a dollar to each of your team members and tell them, "Do what I say, and there's more where that came from"?

5. **When you have a complex problem to untangle, do you**

A) Break out the markers and make notes on a whiteboard?

B) Pray?

C) Build a mind map that mimics the structure of neurons?

6. **When you need to budget a project and you're not sure of the cost of certain items (and can't be sure, due to market conditions or other factors), do you**

   A) Make a wild-assed guess (a WAG)?

   B) Make a swinging wild-assed guess (a SWAG)?

   C) Write up a range estimate?

7. **When you need to speak before groups (or merely with a team member), do you**

   A) Pay special attention to sociolects?

   B) Picture your group wearing nothing but their underwear?

   C) Picture your group wearing nothing but *your* underwear?

8. **When dealing with multiple clients with multiple projects, do you**

   A) Use CRM to track calls, letters, e-mail, and meetings?

   B) Update them daily by phone?

   C) Promise what you can't deliver, then, when they remind you of what you promised, tell them it was just the medication talking?

Want the best answers?

1 - C	5 - C
2 - B	6 - C
3 - B	7 - A
4 - A	8 - A

If you got any of these right—even one—then you're well on your way to herding chickens. If you got more than one right, then you're a promising chicken herder already, and you can read this book to expand your already growing skills. If you got them all right, well, buy this book anyway.

What no one likes, of course, is an overdue and over-budget project, which is precisely what this book will teach you to avoid. And it will show you how to help your team—the essential building block of projects—work together better. So read it, enjoy it, and be sure to send us feedback at our website at http://www.HerdingChickens.com, where you can also download the forms and templates mentioned in the text and find other goodies for your use. (To download the templates, just click the Templates button on the homepage and follow the directions you see on screen. You can also download templates from the Sybex website at http://www.Sybex.com. Just type "herding chickens" in the search box and follow the directions you see on the next page.)

We'd love to hear what you think. We'd love to get to know you. And we'd love to help you run your projects better.

Chapter 1

Building the Killer Project Team

Have you heard one of these gems?

- "There's no I in TEAMWORK."

- "Teamwork, simply stated, is less me and more we."

- "TEAM = Together Everyone Achieves More"

- "A job worth doing is worth doing together."

- "A successful team beats with one heart."

God, they make us want to hurl. This is business, not a Hallmark card, and to get to the top in business—to get to the top in any field—you not only have to accept reality but master it. As far as teams go, that means dealing with egos and cliques and factions and squabbles and squalls. After all, as a project manager (PM) and chicken herder, it's your job to iron out a team's problems and nudge it in the right direction. Teams are simply vital to projects.

But it also means dealing with moments of gorgeous inspiration, times of friendship and collaboration that are nothing less than exquisite. There is, after all, one teamwork quote that we like: "None of us is as smart as all of us." (Thanks to management/leadership author and guru Ken Blanchard for that thought.)

So, in the pages that follow, we've gathered some of the best advice on teamwork for the intelligent PM that we've found in more than four decades of dealing with teams of every stripe, from the highly dysfunctional to the high fliers. We trust you'll enjoy it. But we also urge you to remember the simplest truth of building your project team: Projects are delivered by people, so choose them both—projects and people—wisely.

The Four Types of Teams

Teams are a bit like animals: They come in species, and they're immensely hard to tame, which is why it pays to know what kind of team you have so you'll know how to get the most from it. By and large, we like to break teams down into four types, depending on how team members communicate with one another:

Dysfunctional A dysfunctional team is just what it sounds like: a mess. Team members don't know one another very well, don't talk to one another very well, and certainly don't listen to one another very well. They work as independent agents with little or no coordination between them, barely toeing the leader's line. What's more, this species of team brings projects in over budget and behind schedule (or quite often, not at all), and rarely earns the trust or admiration of other teams in the enterprise. (In fact, sometimes they're scorned.) You'd think this species of team would be well on its way to extinction (they perform so badly that, over time, they degenerate or get disbanded), but in truth they're as common as flies in the forest. It's simply the nature of the beast. When a team first forms, it's burdened by the problems of its members—egos, insecurities, and so on—and they hinder the team's efficiency.

Competitive In the food chain, competitive teams are a step up from their dysfunctional cousins. Team players know each other and know the tasks at hand, and they function with a modicum of coordination. But, like animals that roam in packs, team members are given to competing with one another and trying to establish dominance. Fights for the leader's position are common as alpha males and females assert their territories. Needless to say, this hinders the project's progress and keeps the team, which may be composed of talented people, from coming into its own.

Communicative A communicative team is more evolved. Its members know how to talk to each other and more importantly, they know how to listen. They function with a reasonable degree of cohesion and often have a track record of finished, successful projects. There's a clear and defined leader who runs the pack, and no one bothers to challenge his (or her) supremacy. What's more, buzz about these teams quickly spreads throughout the enterprise, as senior managers and executives sit up and take note of their performance.

Intuitive Think of a school of fish or a flock of birds turning—they do so without effort, perfectly timed, moving and thinking and breathing as one. This is the intuitive team, the highest species of team in the jungle. Its members not only know one another's strengths and foibles like the back of their hand, they know to respect them. With a tried-and-true leader, this team has the universal respect (and sometimes the awe) of other teams in the enterprise, and functions on loyalty and a level of self-knowledge so highly refined that little communication is needed to carry out tasks. These teams make things happen; these teams get things done.

As a PM and team leader, your goal is to build an intuitive team from the ground up. How? The tips in this chapter will help. But even beyond them, remember to use some common sense and follow some basic rules for being a good leader:

Be positive. It's infectious. Your attitude will go a long way with your team. And besides, nobody likes a sourpuss.

Don't micromanage. There's nothing that people hate more than being watched constantly. Give your team members the space they need to do their job and prove their competence.

Never carp. Instead, give sparing, constructive criticism. And couch it in careful terms—no one likes to be told he's wrong.

Value your group's ideas. Chances are they're better than yours. Having ten heads to put on a problem is better than having one.

It's also important to be patient: Becoming an intuitive team takes time and occurs like any other evolution: slowly. As it does, you'll evolve from a dysfunctional team to the other team types until you arrive at the apex. And keep in mind that you don't have much of a choice: The corporate office is like the jungle, and "survival of the fittest" is the word of the day. Either your team evolves to the intuitive level or, in time, you become another part of the fossil record.

··

Writing with Cheap Pens

(Here's an example of a dysfunctional team in action, *with names and dates changed to protect the litigious and innocent.*)

Thank God for management, without whom we'd have no recourse to Bufferin (or hari-kiri). Just months ago a good friend and fine project manager—and cellist extraordinaire—told us a tale of a project team that devolved from intuitive to dysfunctional in a matter of days, thanks to management's lack of communication.

It happened like this: The management at a fine pen company in New York convened a project team to analyze which of their lines of pens had failed in the last five years and why. (An aside, for color: These were exceptional pens, made of silver, platinum, and rhodium, and costing, on the upper end, more than $1000 each. These were the kinds of pens that presidents and prime ministers used to sign bills into law in gilded rooms with senators beside them and cameras before them.). But despite their beauty, not all of these pens sold well. The team was charged with finding a set of financial metrics to define a pen's failure and mapping out ways to avoid such failures in the future.

Like most teams, this one started with all the verve it needed to tackle the problem. In two months they'd evolved to the intuitive level, with team members implicitly knowing each others' needs and working as one towards the project goal. They met for an hour a week for three more months, and at the end of their fifth month, they met with management to present their findings. Little did they know their effective communication with each other did not extend to their communications with management.

The brass, it turned out, was not looking for an objective review of past failures, but a way to scapegoat certain projects for the firm's financial problems. They rejected the team's findings as a whole and sent them packing, back to the drawing board with little or no direction on how to deliver their work.

As a result, the team was so demoralized that its members began to bail, drifting off towards other projects and skipping team meetings. Not only did they not understand their new directives (what there was of them, anyway), they were utterly confused as to why their first piece of work was rejected. The team quickly regressed to the dysfunctional state, and in the end, they never produced another report to give to management.

They did, however, get their revenge, if subtly. For the next year they refused to write anything, even a Post-It note to their boss, with any thing but a cheap ballpoint pen.

Calling Dr. Phil: Using Myers-Briggs Evaluations

Excuse us. Are you an ENTJ, an ESFP, an INTJ, an ESFJ, an INTP, an ENFP, an ISTJ, or an ESTP? Not sure? Not even sure what those acronyms mean?

No problem; we'll educate you. Those bizarre little series of letters are scores on the Myers-Briggs personality test. It's a simple model of personality based on four questions:

- Where do you direct your energy?

- How do you prefer to process information?

- How do you prefer to make decisions?

- How do you prefer to organize your life?

As you can guess, these questions are vital to knowing how a person reacts towards her team members, and how those team members approach a task.

There are three versions of the personality test to help you understand how you and your team members react to each other and how they might tackle project assignments. The first is the *Myers-Briggs Type Indicator (MBTI)*, invented by Isabel Briggs Myers and Katharine C. Briggs. It requires a qualified administrator, called an MBTI Qualified Practitioner, who's almost always a shrink of one shade or another. (Check out www.myersbriggs.org to find out how to become qualified and certified to administer the MBTI.) The MBTI, as it's known, reports your personality using codes like the ones you saw above.

The second test is the *Keirsey Temperament Sorter*, which you can find in a small but popular book named *Please Understand Me* by David Keirsey and Marilyn Bates. It hews closely to the Myers-Briggs questionnaire and can be purchased at most online bookstores. (You can find more information about it at www.keirsey.com.)

The third test is the *Management Team Role-indicator (MTR-i) questionnaire*, which, like the MBTI, must be administered by a good psychologist. It's published by The Test Agency and was developed in an Internet study using more than 20,000 respondents. It reports your work persona or team role, such as Coach, Curator, Explorer, Innovator, Sculptor, or Conductor. As you can guess, it's tailored to your work context and how you interact in teams. You can find more information about the MTR-i at www.16type-suniversity.com/mtri.html.

Now, a note in deference to you skeptics: As with all questionnaires, these are reductive typologies that can clearly be "wrong." There's no way to reduce the complex subtleties of the human psyche to a simple code that tells you all you need to know about how a person reacts in groups. In fact, it's ludicrous to think it can be done. But that's not the value of Myers-Briggs or any of its offshoots.

The true value is what these tests reveal to you about yourself, and what they reveal to your team about how to interact with you. They're *not* a communications nostrum; they're simply a way to find out who's more expressive than others, who prefers hard facts to intuition or gut feelings, who needs a structured work environment, who has an entrepreneur's talent for thriving on chaos, and so on. They're an invaluable tool to see what your team members are made of, and how they'll work together and with you as their leader. Applied at the start of a project, the MBTI, which can be run in an hour as part of your project kickoff meeting, can give you precious insight into your team members' way of doing business.

Now, that said, it's not our goal to turn you into a Ph.D. overnight. And the truth is, we can't. We're no experts in the rarefied realms of psychological testing. But we *can* explain a thing or two about the Myers-Briggs test and what you'll need to know to get the most out of it for your team. (We'll stick with the MBTI, rather than the Keirsey or MTR-i, because MBTI is the oldest of the three and far and away the one most commonly used.)

Let's start with those four questions we mentioned before:

- Where do you direct your energy?

- How do you prefer to process information?

- How do you prefer to make decisions?

- How do you prefer to organize your life?

Where do you direct your energy? This one's easy. If you direct the bulk of your energy to the outer realm of people, activity, and words, you're an Extrovert, or an E. If, on the other hand, you put your mental faculties into the inner realms of ideas, thoughts, and information, shying away from the outer, more social world, then you're an Introvert, or an I. Get the picture?

By and large—and again, we're not trying to encapsulate the whole of the human psyche in a pill-sized paragraph, merely to make a few astute, if general, observations—extroverts are social, expressive, expansive, and tend to put action before thought. Compare them to introverts, who by definition are private, quiet, contemplative, and put thought before action. Introverts may also feel exhausted after intense interactions with other people, the kind you're likely to see in a team on a tight deadline.

Which are you?

How do you prefer to process information? Do you prefer known facts and familiar terms, or do you prefer to explore new patterns and meanings in data? If it's the former, it's called *Sensing*, or S in the Myers-Briggs scheme. If it's the latter, it's called *Intuition*, or N. (Why not I? To avoid confusion with Introvert, of course.)

Let's explain this in more depth. The Sensing mode is focused on the present, on tangible reality, on seeing what is and not what might come to pass. On the contrary, the Intuition preference puts greater weight on insight and the future, on what could be and not on what is. At its extreme, sensing can focus so much on the here and now that it fails to see the realm of possibility. Intuition, by contrast, can focus so much on possibility that it fails to see the reality of the present.

People who rely on sensing tend to like facts, evidence, practicality, and realism. The intuitives among us, on the other hand, are into possibilities, novelties, aspirations, change, and idealism.

How do you prefer to make decisions? Do you make decisions on the basis of logic or objective considerations, or do you decide an issue based on your personal values? If it's the first, it's called *Thinking* in the Myers-Briggs scheme and denoted by T; if it's the second, it's called *Feeling*, denoted by—guess what?—an F.

This one's rather easy to define. Thinkers are objective analysts. They're often logical—sometimes coldly so—and they decide on principle and take the long-term view. By contrast, feelers are more subjective and empathic, more personal, have a greater appreciation for the views of other participants, and take an immediate view of the situation.

How do you like to organize your life? Do you prefer to live in a structured way, with a preference for making strong decisions, or do you prefer to live in a bit of flux, keeping your options open?

If you like the structured life, you're said to have *Judgment*, or J, in the Myers-Briggs typology. If, on the other hand, you like a more flexible life, open to pleasures as you find them, you're said to have *Perception*, or P.

Someone whose preference is Judgment likes to decide things, often ahead of time—what to do, where to go, what to say, and so forth. As a result, they appear organized or, taken to the extreme, even rigid. They like structure, firmness, planning, control. Those with a preference for Perception like to learn or experience new things. They're more comfortable when they keep their options open and their ear to the ground. As a result, they can appear flexible to their friends and colleagues. Inquisitive, they like to explore and excite; they like spontaneity.

Extrovert-Introvert. Sensing-Intuition. Thinking-Feeling. Judgment-Perception. In all there are sixteen combinations...which are you?

ESTJ (Extrovert, Sensing, Thinking, Judgment): The Supervisor
The ESTJ is an extrovert, so he draws his energy from those around

him, from the outside world of people and actions. He also prefers to use logic to deal with facts and the present, and keeps his life organized in a logical way. Practical and pragmatic, the ESTJ is likely to try known and trusted solutions for problems, which he'll attack in a fairly impersonal manner. And he's a detail man, preferring to hone in on the specifics of a project rather than spend time on strategy.

INFP (Introvert, Intuition, Feeling, Perception): The Healer An introvert, the INFP looks to the future, to possibilities, and decides on personal values. She leads a flexible life, quiet and adaptable, but only up to a point. The INFP can surprise people with a sudden rigidity when her values are violated. With a bent for creativity, she has a hidden warmth for people and a desire to see others grow.

ESFP (Extrovert, Sensing, Feeling, Perception): The Performer The ESFP is an extrovert—he takes his energy from the outside world of people and actions. Given to sensing, not intuition, he prefers to deal with facts. He also deals in the present and likes friendships. (In fact, he tends to make new friends easily.) Flexible, he takes life as it comes, nearly to the point of impulsivity. He also has a taste for the urgent problem and its solution. The ESFP is a known firefighter, and a damn good one at that.

INTJ (Introvert, Intuition, Thinking, Judgment): The Mastermind
This introvert tends to decide things on the basis of impersonal analysis. He's a rather organized strategist who contemplates life's long-term goals; in fact, his life may be organized to meet them. He's skeptical and often critical, both of self and others, and has a nose for deficiencies in quality and competence alike. INTJs often have big brains and can apply them to details relevant to larger strategies.

ESFJ (Extrovert, Sensing, Feeling, Judgment): The Provider This extrovert likes facts but makes decisions based on personal values. Warm and outgoing, she's a people person who looks to maintain harmony with colleagues and friends, and doesn't always warm to conflict or critique. Her strong sense of duty and loyalty makes her want to be of service, and she has a genuine desire to help others.

INTP (Introvert, Intuition, Thinking, Perception): The Architect An introvert, the Architect decides questions on a logical basis. She likes a flexible life and goes with the flow. She's quiet, possibly detached, and reasonably adaptable. She'll often experiment or change things to see if they can be improved, and tends to operate best when her intellect, most often large, is put to the solution of complex problems.

ENFP (Extrovert, Intuition, Feeling, Perception): The Champion The Champion, an extrovert by nature, prefers to think about future possibilities over the here and now, especially where people are concerned, and decides things based on personal values. She's creative, insightful, and may sometimes neglect details and planning. But she enjoys work that involves experimentation and variety, so long as it's working towards a general goal.

ISTJ (Introvert, Sensing, Thinking, Judgment): The Inspector The Inspector is more than an introvert: He's a hard-nosed dealer in facts who likes to make decisions after he's considered all the options. He likes to organize his life on a logical basis. He's quiet, serious, and tends to be well-prepared. He's a keen observer, a watcher and listener who won't always express his thoughts, but has a strong sense of goals and works hard to meet them.

ESTP (Extrovert, Sensing, Thinking, Perception): The Promoter
This extrovert swims in pools of facts and makes decisions on a purely logical basis. He also leads a flexible life that consists of activities that interest him. A problem solver, he's action-oriented, so much so that he can be impulsive. He likes trouble-shooting but at times can neglect follow-through. That said, he's a wonderful team member to have in situations that need organizing and solving.

INFJ (Introvert, Intuition, Feeling, Judgment): The Counselor An introvert, the Counselor sees the future and possibilities in people, maintains a private sense of purpose in life, and works to fulfill that goal. Brimming with empathy, he shows a quiet concern for people. This in turn makes him a good manager: He'd like to help his colleagues grow, and his insight—which sometimes remains unexpressed—is often impeccable.

ENFJ (Extrovert, Intuition, Feeling, Judgment): The Teacher The Teacher is an extrovert. He's intuitive and prefers to think in terms of possibilities in the future. He also looks to develop and maintain stable relationships with people he likes, as well as promote personal growth in others. Highly sociable and expressive of feelings, they can find conflict and critique difficult, but tend to work best with other people, not alone.

ISTP (Introvert, Sensing, Thinking, Perception): The Crafter An introvert, the Crafter deals in facts and logical decisions, the here and now, but keeps her life flexible and takes things as they come. Quiet and detached, she's adaptable up to a point. She also has a talent for solving organizational problems, and may be very curious about why things work. While she can seem impulsive, she can also produce surprising—and surprisingly good—ideas and unpredictable, often unorthodox solutions.

ENTJ (Extrovert, Intuition, Thinking, Judgment): The Field Marshall This extrovert likes to look to the future and consider the realm of possibility. (But she won't leap before she looks; she'll consider the results of her actions before she takes them.) She tends to be logical and controlling, organizing systems and even people to meet her goals. ENTJs are often executives and directors; their approach, not surprisingly, is often called impersonal. On occasion, they may appear intolerant of people who don't seem to be good at what they do.

ISFP (Introvert, Sensing, Feeling, Perception): The Composer A known introvert, the Composer likes to deal with facts and people and decides the questions of life and work based on a set of personal values. She's adaptable, she's quiet, she's friendly, and she enjoys the company of others one on one or in small numbers. This person enjoys the present and tends to dislike conflict.

ENTP (Extrovert, Intuition, Thinking, Perception): The Inventor The Inventor is an extrovert who looks to the future and the realm of possibility. He tends to decide issues on a logical basis free of emotions, and likes to increase his own competence and skills. An ingenious problem solver, he enjoys a good argument, likes to promote change, and operates best in situations where creative effort drives new solutions.

ISFJ (Introvert, Sensing, Feeling, Judgment): The Protector An introvert, the Protector likes dealing with facts, but decides on personal values. He leads an organized life, and is quiet, serious, and concerned for the feelings of others, often to the point of solicitude. He tends to be loyal and conscientious, and prefers to be of practical service to the group. Like most, he dislikes confrontation and conflict, but he's willing to risk it when others' feelings are at stake.

As a PM you can run Myers-Briggs at the start of your projects, using your team as lab rats. The most effective way is to bring in a MBTI Qualified Practitioner for the first team meeting. He'll be able to run the test and talk about the different personality types. And while it won't tell you all you need to know about your team members, it will give you some basic insight into how they think, feel, and act, and how they're apt to act towards one another—how, that is, they'll work as a team. It can also tell you who's good at what.

An example: Say you've got a problem that needs a novel solution. Assign an Inventor (ENTP) or a Crafter (ISTP) to handle the job. Both thrive on ingenious problem-solving; they're good with Gordian Knots. If, on the other hand, you've got a large, messy project that needs to be organized and whipped into shape, call on a Field Marshall (ENTJ). These little Napoleons know how to regiment people and resources alike (hence their name). Architects (INTP) are good at big, complex problems that need fine-tuning—it's the nature of their intellect to tweak and tinker. And Counselors (INFJ) have a talent for issues that need a touch of tact and empathy.

Hence you can use Myers-Briggs to fine-tune your team dynamics, assigning people to tasks based on their type. What's more, team members—after taking the Myers-Briggs test—will learn something about their own makeup and the makeup of their colleagues. And in the end, that can only foster the birth of killer teams.

The '96 Olympics Personality Challenge

Ana O. was the daughter and granddaughter of Olympians. Her father medaled in the high jump—a bronze—as a young man, and her grandfather, competing for Mexico, brought home gold in his day when he beat a Finn and a Swede in the 100 meter hurdles. So they were overly pleased when Ana's first assignment as a newly-minted PM was to the '96 Atlanta games. Her task? Plan and run a ceremony for one of the rowing events.

There was, of course, a problem. The local Olympic committee had convened a project team of 16 members from different firms (only two were from Ana's firm) and some from different cultures. (After all, this *was* the Olympics.) And as a result, the team was finding it hard to communicate with any degree of efficiency.

Green but determined, Ana sought the advice of a senior PM in her firm. The PM was an advocate of using the Myers-Briggs Type Indicator for team building, and he suggested she call a meeting to conduct the MBTI test and share the results with her team. She did, and it was an effective session that showed her diverse team the ins and outs of different personality types.

But rather than end it there, with a simple exercise conducted in group, Ana took it further. She had placards made for each team member that displayed his or her type: ENTJ, ISTP, and so on, along with a cartoon of each type. For the next three months, until everyone grew comfortable working together, team members displayed the placards somewhere on their desk, so that other members would know exactly which communication styles to use with one another.

Forming, Storming, Norming, Performing

Alas, as theories go, this one's not our own. But as with all good theories, it's worth knowing nonetheless.

In 1965, a man named Dr. Bruce Tuckman read through 50 or so studies on the way groups become teams. (Don't ask us why; maybe he had too much time on his hands.) He found that teams, for better or worse, pass through four stages on their way to cohesion: *Forming*, *Storming*, *Norming*, and *Performing*.

As a PM, it's important for you to know the stages so you can know which one your team is in—or mired in, as the case may be—and plot a strategy to find your way out. And it's important for your team to know the stages as well, so they know that what they're doing and feeling and the way they're reacting to one another is perfectly normal.

> **Forming** This is the first stage in the team-building dynamic. It's the polite stage where team members get to know one another for the first time. By and large it's a time of high excitement and optimism, but beware: It's also a time for mild anxiety and suspicion. *Why are we here? What are we doing?* Team members may cautiously test the boundaries of good behavior and, as part and parcel of that testing, test the power of the group's leader as well.
>
> While there can be pride in being chosen for the team, attachment to the team, at least for now, is still tentative. The team itself is embryonic: It's deciding what information needs to be gathered and how it should be given out. It's deciding who gets what information and why, and goals and metrics for performance are just coming into being. Because there's so much going on logistically, the team gets little done towards its goals at this point. And that, frankly, is quite normal.
>
> **Storming** This is the stormy stage, the hardest phase of team growth. Now that members have met one another and begun the initial tasks of coalescence, they begin to inject themselves—and their egos—into the process of pushing the project forward. Personal agendas run rampant. Members begin to realize the full range of tasks that lie ahead;

invariably they see that those tasks are more diverse and difficult than planned. Arguments may abound: How should we proceed? Who should do what? Collaborations are rare and rarely work.

And it gets worse. Team members may resist the tasks they're assigned. They may resist you. Their attitudes towards the team and towards its chance for success may swing wildly. They may become defensive, competitive, or dysfunctional. Cliques may form. They may question the wisdom of those who formed the project; they may question the wisdom—and rights—of the PM. Expect jealousy and disunity.

But underneath these black currents of ill will and turmoil are signs of hope. Team members are beginning to understand one another. They're moving towards Norming.

Norming The breakthrough. The team begins to find its focus. It begins to build enthusiasm; over time, that reaches an apex and the team wants to go beyond its scope. Old wounds heal. Competitions morph into loyalties. Members begin to accept the team and their roles within it; the ground rules—simply words on paper before this phase—become sacrosanct. Emotional conflicts begin to fade.

Lo and behold, critique can be expressed constructively. Friendships emerge across cliques, and a sense of cohesion begins to build. Goals are shared across the team, and boundaries begin to be respected. Not only do you, the PM, begin to *see* progress, you begin to *feel* it, daily, in your bones.

Performing Nirvana. (Well, not quite. But from the point of view of team building, you're approaching enlightenment.) The team has found its stride and can really begin to run. Team members have finally learned each others' strengths and deficits, come to accept them, and learned to work with them. Goals are wholly agreed upon, and there's a sense of loyalty to the team.

By this point the team is in fighting form. It's a cohesive unit, and it's effective, as strong as Alexander's army.

So which stage is your team in? In fact it's not uncommon for teams to move back and forth between stages. A team that's chugging along in the Performing stage may jump back to Forming when new members sign on. A team that's Norming may find itself Storming when it's unable to meet a key goal, and so on.

If you're Forming, enjoy the honeymoon...Storming's on the way. If you're Storming, know that it won't last; like adolescence, it's just a normal, rowdy phase of development. (Though we do offer a caveat: We've seen groups that spend scads of time—abnormal amounts—in Storming. If you're one of them, own up to it and find a way out. If not, you'll come in over budget, behind schedule, and weak and tired at the finish line.) If you're Norming, enjoy those first nips of progress, and if you're Performing, give us a call and let us know how you got there. We're always up for a good story.

How to Fire a Team Member

What's the best way to fire a team member? Not to fire him at all, of course.

We'll explain. From time to time you'll request or inherit a team member from another part of the firm who turns out to be a dud. Perhaps he can't type. Perhaps he can't tie his shoes. Whatever. The bottom line is he's a dolt and you need to get rid of him—fast. But how?

You could, of course, confront him and duke it out. If that's your chosen course of action, you might as well sell tickets to the fight and set up concessions. (Popcorn is always good, and hot dogs, don't forget the relish, go well with a nice conflict.) After all, the entire office will know about it anyway; it's called the grapevine, and it works faster than you can say "gossip." And don't forget to factor in the effects it will have on office morale. Whenever you drop anyone from a team—except, perhaps, for the worst of parasites—team morale suffers.

So go the second route. Issue a recall, or to be more accurate, have a recall issued. In confidence, go back to the group leader that sent you this sorry excuse for a biped and broker a deal. Explain that it's not working out; that, despite best efforts, so-and-so is not working on your team, but to save face and avoid an incident, could you please "recall" him to his prior team so it *appears* as if he's being asked to return to his former home and not being asked to leave his new one?

Of course, the group leader you appeal to may be unwilling to help. But if you have some tact and you're willing to give some *quid* for some *quo*, there's a good chance you'll be able to swing a deal and fire a team member without having to fire him at all.

A note in closing: There are times when you simply *have* to fire a team member outright. His performance is so poor, his attitude so corrosive, that he's no good on any team, including yours. He's simply a cipher. You can't trade him off to another team because no one will take him. If that's the case, start to document his failings, and be meticulous. Note every error and mishap. Then, proof in hand, take it to the brass and request his dismissal. Because we live in a litigious culture, it's hard to fire someone outright, so you'll need to arm your executives with the data they need to justify their move.

You're Kinda Fired

His name was Lukas and he was a Czech architect of some renown, most of it gained as a young man when he designed, at the mere age of 30, a radical museum of modern art in São Paolo. But in the last two decades his career had faltered and he failed to get the commissions he sought, leaving him by and large an embittered man.

At 50 and needing money, he took a job as the project architect on the construction of a new sports arena in the deep South, where he supervised a team of 12 designers—badly. He was abusive and highly intolerant of errors; perhaps worse, he suffered no fools, a trait of patience that's often required of those who work on large projects where the team is a grab bag of talents.

Within a month his team of designers was at their wit's end, tired and ready to bolt their jobs for greener pastures. In desperation, they met in a Chinese restaurant, where they decided, over cashew chicken and spring rolls, with paper placemats of the Chinese Zodiac before them, to complain at length to the PM.

In turn, the PM went to the firm that assigned Lukas to the project and asked them to reassign him. They did, framing the new assignment as a promotion to avoid any negative stigma. Then they assigned a new architect to head the team of designers for the sports arena. The result? The arena had a world-class design, and friction in the project team was reduced to nil.

Learning (and Living) the IGT Rule

In the precise world of arithmetic, $1 + 1 = 2$, always. Likewise, $1 + 1 + 1 = 3$, and $1 + 1 + 1 + 1 = 4$. The whole is always the sum of its parts.

But in the amorphous mathematics of groups, $1 + 1$ can be less than 2, and $1 + 1 + 1$ can be less than 3. How? It's really quite simple.

Take a person, a single person, and put him alone in a room with a task, say, sorting widgets. Alone, he can sort 100 widgets per hour. Now put another person in the same room and have them sort widgets together. The result? Not what you'd expect. Do they sort 200 widgets per hour ($1 + 1 = 2$)? No. More like 150. Maybe 125. Why? Because they talk to each other (and hence lose time), argue (and hence lose time), and coordinate and sometimes fumble or drop widgets (and hence lose time).

Add a third person and the problems of coordination grow more severe. True, there are more hands to do more work, and hence the *potential* for greater output exists, but there are also more problems that arise as those hands begin to interact. So in the strange math of groups, $1 + 1 = 1.5$. And $1 + 1 + 1 = 2.5$, and so on.

But over time, something happens. Those people in that room begin to develop rules. They begin to coordinate their efforts and communicate. They begin to standardize their movements and motions. They evolve a set of best practices. They may even evolve a hierarchy, with a defined structure and a head. They resolve their disputes and begin to learn the ins and outs of one another's personalities. In short, they begin to gel—that is, they begin to become a team.

The result? Output shoots up. At first, they sort 200 widgets per hour. Then 300. Then more, so that soon they're sorting a startling 1000 widgets per hour, more than any three people could possibly sort alone. And yet again a strange math evolves, this time for the good. Now, the whole is more than the sum of its parts. Now, $1 + 1 + 1 = 10$.

Hence the *Individuals Groups Teams (IGT) rule*. We start alone with an output equal to one, then form groups whose output is less than the sum of its parts (or, to be more accurate, less than the potential output of the sum of its parts). Only with time, training, and the application of talent do we form into teams, whose output is more than the sum of its parts.

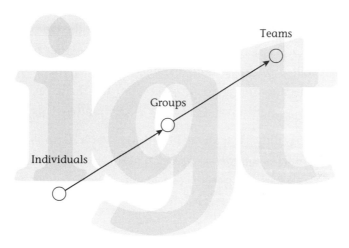

So the question, of course, is which phase is your team in? Doubtless you've assembled a group of people to attack a project and drive it home, but are they truly a team? Do you have a well-defined structure with an agreed-upon head? (Most groups don't; all teams do.) Do you have standards and procedures and even best practices? (Groups simply reinvent the wheel; teams keep it well-oiled.) Do you have strong communication and communication channels? (Groups fight amongst themselves; teams talk to one another.) Have your conflicts been resolved, or, at the least, do you have a defined method of conflict resolution? (Groups bicker; teams work through their problems.)

If, as you read this, you find that your project "team" is more of a project group, take heart. Teams, like diamonds, take time and pressure to form. No time, no pressure, no team. Remember: The role of the PM and chicken herder is truly one of a survivalist: Your job is to help your group survive—to help them adhere and cohere—until they become a team. For that you need little more than wit, wisdom, perseverance, and a bit of luck.

Gilligan's Island

Sometimes it takes a boat to make a team evolve. Four years ago a PM named James N. headed a project team that was assembled to develop a piece of software at a large telco. Sadly, the team was truly dysfunctional. Its members had never worked together before, and infighting, cliques, and personal agendas reigned supreme. There was no clear understanding of the project scope, and the team, such as it was, had been languishing for close to three months.

But James was crafty. He rented a boat and took all 20 members of his team to a small but deserted island with nothing on it but flies—nothing, that is, but flies and a set of clues to a unique scavenger hunt that he'd laid out the day before. He left them stranded and took the boat sailing.

The team of 20 was split into four teams of five and made to search the island using the clues as guides. The prize? A cell phone, without which they were unable to call James to return with the boat and take them home.

With such an incentive to cooperate, they began to communicate, to learn each others' ins and outs and work less as a group of soloists and more as a symphony. The result? They covered the island and found the phone in two hours. They called James, who returned with the boat and a catered lunch (complete with shrimp and lobster, natch) and took the entire team sailing on the bay.

Back in the office, the team began to evolve. They identified their project's goals and deadlines, wrote a firm statement of scope with milestones, and outlined each person's responsibilities. Lo and behold, they began to cohere, and quickly left the dysfunctional stage and grew, over time, into an intuitive team. They found ways to combine their unique talents, set aside their group mentalities and cliques, and write a killer app that rocked.

Gasp! IPRs and Audits

Audits, as we all know, are roughly as fun as root canal. But *independent project reviews (IPRs)* are birds of a different feather. They're kinder, gentler reviews of your project team, designed to hurt no one. In fact, if you run them right, IPRs can be useful tools in your project arsenal.

We'll deal with audits in a bit. For now, an IPR, as the name implies, is a review of your project and its status by a team of experts (often they do nothing but IPRs, so they've honed their craft well) who have nothing to do with your organization. They're a set of outside eyes, sharp, eager, and often hired by you or a project's owner to give you their unbiased thoughts on how you're doing.

Why bother? After all, at the start of your project you established a set of metrics and other milestones to measure your progress and judge your own aptitude, no? True, but those are metrics that *you've* set, and set in your favor—otherwise put, they're biased towards you to begin with. An IPR brings a truly outside perspective to your project; it rids you of internal bias completely. (Unless, of course, you slip the IPR team a little something under the table. But we advise against that.)

Of course, there are other reasons to bring in some outside guns to size you up. Consider this: Your team is already stretched to capacity just to meet their regular reporting deadlines. How are they going to conduct a thorough review? With what resources? You just don't have the time and the people to review the data, do the interviews, crunch the numbers, and the like. What's more—and this gets back to the issue of bias—the people you do have are too close to the material to judge it well.

So enter the IPR team. At your request they'll review key reports, read key documents, do key interviews, and run key benchmarks against PM best practices. And if they're any good, they'll include in their final report a forecast of the total cost and time required to complete the project, not to mention variance and root cause analysis.

And they'll bring with them a few benefits:

- IPRs reduce the owner's risk—and yours, the PM's. No longer will the owner have to rely solely on the PM as his sole or most crucial source of information; he'll have an independent, outside voice to whisper in his ear. And likewise, the PM, used to relying on his team or key members thereof, will have a useful backstop to ensure the information she gets from them is good.

- The IPR will also point out—politely and constructively—where you've gone wrong and how you can remedy it. And while that may sting a little (PMs, we know, have their pride too), better to know where the fault lines in your project lie before the earthquake hits than to learn their location when the ground starts to rumble.

- An IPR can point out what your team needs. If, for example, you've been pushing for a third network printer for two months but your pleas have fallen on deaf ears, a recommendation from an outside party—the IPR team—may be just the ammo you need to get heard.

So how do you get an IPR? There are firms who do nothing but IPRs, and even some who specialize in IPRs in certain fields (software development, construction, and so on). Just Google them. (For those of you not entirely sure what that means, shame on you! Get yourself to the Web, go to the Google search engine at www.Google.com, and search for "independent project review.")

The wise PM will schedule IPRs for large, long projects at regular intervals in her project's duration, say, once every quarter, six months, or yearly. Fees vary from firm to firm depending on the nature of the project they'll have to analyze and the amount of work it requires.

Now on to *audits*, evil, evil audits. Audits take place only when there's blood in the water. Where IPRs are positive, audits are negative. Where IPRs look to the future, audits look back—with a vengeance. Where IPRs look for inefficiency and suggest solutions, audits look for mistakes and cast blame. IPRs, like a shot of insulin, happen to living, breathing projects to stabilize and fortify them. Audits cut up a cadaver.

If your project is in an audit, then something has gone deadly wrong. Chances are the project's owners are fighting among themselves, and litigation is either imminent or already upon you. Perhaps you've already done some time on the witness stand, or perhaps you're about to. Either way, an audit's been called to pick over the bones of your project and bury it in the sand.

That said, the only question is how to protect yourself and your team from an audit. And the answer is: You may not have to. Or rather, you may have already done so. If you've followed project management's best practices and been careful to document every step of your project—every change request, every budget addition, every turnover in personnel—you've insulated yourself and your team from the damage of the audit, bite and bark alike. By their very nature, audits rely on a paper trail. The better yours is, the better off you—and your team—will be. And don't forget the value of the IPR: Planning one in the first place can help you avoid an audit altogether.

Training Newbies, Using Mentors

It's a sad fact, but true: You'll likely inherit your project team (along with your project, for that matter), and as such, you'll inherit a sundry bunch of folks with skills that range from adept to expert and every shade in between. You'll have everyone from *newbies* to old hands. The question, of course, is what do you do with such a motley mix (besides bang your head against a wall)?

One of the simple answers is to invest in a hefty dollop of *on-the-job training (OJT)* to boost the skills of the newbies up a rank or two. How? Start with the basics: gatherings, officially led trainings, and workshops.

- Weekly Lunch 'n Learns can offer an informal environment where your more seasoned team members—indeed, some of your subject matter experts (SMEs), whom we'll discuss later in this chapter— can share their knowledge over tuna salad or tofu. (Pizza is always good, too: It brings people running.)

- There's always the Project Management Institute (PMI), brimming with online education at www.pmi.org (for a small fee, of course).

- Consider some one-day workshops. They won't take your people out of the loop for long, but they will leave them with a heavy dose of new knowledge that can pay dividend upon dividend in the future.

In fact, the smart chicken herder knows to budget training as a line item in every large project and most small projects she runs. After all, one way to define a manager—and one that's accepted by thousands, if not millions, of managers across the globe—is simply as a person who helps others below her come into their own, to grow as workers whose output (and outlook) improves daily. What better way to help them grow than to help them find the training they need?

But truth be told, OJT only goes so far. The real question is how you get the senior members of your team—the ones with skills to spare— to share those skills with their juniors. How do you get them, that is, to cross-pollinate?

Enter the *mentor*. According to the American Heritage Dictionary, this word means "a wise and trusted counselor or teacher;" as a verb it means "to serve as a counselor or teacher, especially in occupational settings." It also has quite a little history, dating back to the time of the Greeks and Homer's *Odyssey*. In it, Athena, disguised as a man named Mentor, guides Odysseus' son Telemachus in the search for his father. Hence the meaning of the word *mentor* as *guide* and by extension, *counselor* or *teacher*.

Now, Greek lessons aside, what does this have to do with your projects, you ask? Simple: Part of your role as a project manager is to bring about the cross-pollination of ideas among the members of your project team. And there's no better way to do it than to promote, in an informal, unstructured way, student-mentor bonds between newbies and SMEs or other senior members of your project team.

Teach the Teachers

Don't forget that mentoring—teaching of any kind, for that matter— is an art, and one that takes practice. You can't simply assign a mentor to a newbie on your team and expect sparks to fly. You have to remember to teach the teachers, too.

How, and where? Consider the SME meeting discussed later in this chapter. Use this gathering as a chance to let your senior team members and SMEs know that you'll be pairing them informally with junior colleagues in an effort to improve their colleagues' skills. Then open up the floor to a discussion on how to do it best.

How do you promote student-mentor bonds? The first step is to know, with some degree of precision, what skills your team members have and what skills your team members need. The easy part is learning what skills they have. Simply conduct a *skills assessment* (or *self-assessment*) for each. Find out who knows Russian; who's done focus groups; who's got a handle on PeopleSoft; who gets ROI and its calculation; who knows all about search engine marketing; or who's dealt with the press.

Then, by intuition and observation, begin to learn who's lacking in which skills. Perhaps you have a team member who knows little or nothing about project management. You can take him under your wing. Perhaps you have another team member whose presentation skills are lacking. Here, clearly, you'll need to pair him with a mentor who speaks with the ease of Clinton and the power of Reagan, and let it rub off. And so forth. Remember: Your team is your team's best asset. Be smart. Let them train one another. Let them mentor one another. And let them grow as a team.

What About Your Project Intranet?

Do you have a project *intranet*? If not, then get off your duff and get one, by hook or by crook. It can be made into a goldmine.

A prime example: Once you've deeply surveyed your team for their skill sets, and know, for example, who's a whiz with PowerPoint macros and who's got experience with Costa Rican contractors, put the information online *and make it searchable*. That way, you're not the only one responsible for your team's cross-pollination of knowledge. When a team member has an issue that's over his head or out of his league, he can simply hop online, search the intranet, and find out which of his colleagues, if any, have experience in that field.

Turnover: It's Gonna Happen

God, we hate to lose good talent. A good worker—the kind you can trust, depend on, call on, the kind you can leave alone—is worth her weight in gold. Losing one is like having a tooth pulled. A front tooth, no less.

But the truth is you'll always lose talent on your projects. It's a fact of life you can't help. In fact, you may be the very talent you lose—on some projects, even the PM has to go from time to time. Take, for example, large-scale construction jobs where there's one PM to manage the basic structure (we're talking foundation, walls, and so forth) and a second who comes in when the structure's done to manage the interior finishings (the light fixtures and such). Often these shifts from one PM to another are determined well in advance, at the start of the project as part of the project plan.

If you've got a project that runs for two, three, or five years, there's bound to be scads of project turnover. As a rule of thumb, you're lucky if good talent stays on the project for two years. If you're one of those rare people who can keep good talent for more than two years, well, hallelujah.

That said, we'll break down the turnover you see in your projects into two different types: involuntary on the one hand, voluntary on the other. Perhaps a better way to phrase this is unplanned and planned.

No one can stop unplanned turnover. Sadly, there are times when workers—even the best—are run over by beer trucks, or have to leave the project team in undue haste when Aunt Tilly dies and leaves them a fortune. (Laugh if you will, but this happened to us before: A valued worker left one of our projects when a distant uncle died and left her a mint in Fabergé eggs.) So buck up and bear it. There's nothing you can do to stop this simple fact of life but pray, and even that bears uncertain results.

Voluntary or planned turnover is an altogether different animal, and a welcome change. When does it happen? As discussed above, when a PM is phased out in favor of another at a crucial—but planned—juncture in the project. Or perhaps you have a contract worker whose contract expires in two months. Since he's let you know that he's unavailable after that (sadly, another gig calls), you have the time and inclination to plan for his departure.

Since you have time to plan for his departure, you also have time to plan for his replacement, and there's no safer way to do this than having a first-rate *project control manual (PCM)* or *project library*, whether it's planned or unplanned turnover at issue. Why? When the replacement arrives—we'll name him Elvis—he can abscond to a quiet room with binders in hand and start to read. In the PCM, Elvis can learn how to handle change requests, time extensions, letters of notification, design deficiencies, *requests for information (RFIs)*, and more.

From your project library he'll read old meeting minutes, reports, budgets, timelines, org charts, changes in org charts, project objectives, initial schedules, new schedules, future schedules under review…in short, anything and everything he needs to come up to speed in no time flat. (This applies to unplanned turnover as well. If you need to bring someone in quickly to fill a void from a sudden absence in your team, there's no better way to bring him current than to sit him down with the PCM and have him read.)

And what's more, with planned turnover, you can schedule overlaps between incoming and outgoing personnel. Otherwise put, Elvis and the man he's replacing can spend a week together, one learning the other's job.

Absence Makes the Heart Grow Fonder

Wires. This book was born in the wires between Atlanta and Miami and San Francisco. Why? Because its authors, Dan Bradbary and David Garrett, live in the first two of those cities respectively, and its editors, Heather O'Connor and Leslie Light, live in the third. What's more, Dan and Dave have never met Heather and Leslie, merely talked with them by phone and e-mail. And that, friends, is what you call a virtual team.

Let's define that term. A *virtual team (VT)* is a team in disparate locations that rarely if ever meets, but works with all the finesse of an on-site team that meets every day. In fact, and in the extreme, a VT can meet round the clock. How? Take, for example, the virtual team that a software giant had formed that consisted of three groups: one in the U.S., one in Europe, and one in India. Tasked with software development, they passed around the source code in eight-hour shifts from the U.S. to Europe to India, so it was never *not* being worked on, 24 hours a day.

VTs have their benefits. No longer bound by geography, you can hire the best people, the best talent, location be damned. What's more, workers tend to be more productive in their own settings, whether that's at home or in their own office space. And that means you'll pay less for rent and infrastructure than you would in a "standard" office.

But there's a dark side to the virtual team as well: absenteeism, overload, loafing, and low commitment from certain team members. For better or worse, co-location is still the preferred way to work, just because of the nature of human nature. We prefer proximity. We like closeness. And to quote an old saw, "trust needs touch." Teams thrive on trust, which grows fastest when you can see (and yes, touch) those you're supposed to trust.

That said, you may find yourself working in virtual teams for part or even all of a project's duration. If so, we have a few words of advice for you:

- VTs need technology like fish need water. So don't be content to merely know *about* the technology or know enough to get by. *Know* the technology, back and forth. Remember: As team leader, you set the tone for everyone below you. If you act like a Luddite, don't expect your colleagues to do much better. And in virtual teams, that can be deadly. Consider this: If you spend merely 5 minutes a day looking for lost e-mail (and most of us spend more), that's 25 minutes per week, or 100 minutes per month for 1200 minutes per year. That's 20 hours, or half a work week, lost to a technical glitch you could easily tame with a bit more knowledge.

- You'll also need a high degree of technical literacy among team members. Now is not the time to seek or hire those who think a CD drive is a cup holder.

- Remember to make the most of simple technologies: e-mail with attachments, teleconferencing, and instant messaging. And don't shy away from the snazzier, jazzier stuff: intranets, extranets, and the like. Curious? Get your feet wet at www.intranets.com. This site lets you and your project team share documents, calendars, contacts and tasks, have online discussions, build database apps, run an audio conference, run opinion polls, manage expense reports, and post announcements, all for dollars a day. Best of all, it's blindingly easy. Even your parents could use it.

- As the PM on a virtual team, you're more than the team leader—you're the team communicator. You'll have to hold the team together, no small task when the team can't see one another from day to day. Bear in mind that some PMs spend as much as a third of their time on the phone, binding their teams together like glue.

- Don't forget to meet from time to time—in fact, as often as your pocketbook (and the rules of efficiency) permit. Remember, "trust needs touch," and there's value in doing business the old-fashioned way: face to face. If you can't meet, find a way to personalize the virtual experience. To wit, post team members' photos on your intranet, so people have a way to put a face with the voice they hear daily on the phone.

- Videoconference. It ain't what it used to be. Now it's simple, cheap, and easy. (For more info on videoconferencing, see Chapter 5, "The Perfect Meeting.")

- Don't stint on the quality of your communications equipment. If you need to shave pennies from your budget, find someplace else to do it. Good VTs need the best technology they can possibly afford.

- More than with a co-located team, VTs need a strong set of written performance metrics: goals, objectives, project specs, and the like. You won't be face to face with your team every day, so you'll need to know you're all on the same page.

And last, find workers who can handle a high degree of autonomy. After all, that's just what you plan to give them. Be sure they'll give you back what you need in return.

Working with SMEs

Newsflash: We don't know jack about JavaScript or cures for neuropathic pain. Guess what? We've never bothered to bone up on the finer points of product packaging or learn the ins and outs of pollution control in power plants. And frankly, we don't give a damn about non-Euclidian numbers or combinatory geometry or international copyrights. Why? Because we have lives, thank you very much.

Problem is, the outcome of your project could turn on subjects as rarefied as these, and there comes a time in the life of every large project (and most small ones, too) when you need an expert's touch, someone who knows the ins and outs of amortizing rental agreements as well as you know the plot line of *The Sopranos*.

Enter the *subject matter experts (SMEs)* (pronounced *shmees*). SMEs are just what they sound like, armies of men and women whose job is to know tiny corners of human knowledge with such depth and breadth that you, thankfully, don't have to. But you do have to worry about working with SMEs, since

- They're often highly intelligent.

- Like most of the world's highly intelligent humans, they have definite thoughts on how to run a project, and those thoughts may not gel with your own.

- Owing to their years of study, high discipline, and advanced training, some of them resemble Yoda.

The truth is, your project may have as many as a dozen SMEs tasked to it, from finance, IT, legal, engineering, and other disciplines. You'll need a way to draw all that brainpower into the open air in a way that vaguely resembles efficiency. What's more, you'll need to do it in a way that cuts down on conflict, since big brains carry with them big egos. And last, you'll need to do it in a way that moves your project forward towards that blessed day called project completion.

With that in mind, we've assembled a tip or two on working with SMEs:

Round 'em up and make 'em meet. Have a SME meeting. In fact, do it shortly after the project kickoff meeting. Invite only your SMEs and plan to spend half an hour or so together (no more—SMEs can have short attention spans) with a loose agenda. Let them introduce themselves to each other and explain their specialties, and most importantly, how those specialties will relate to the project at hand. Even better, let them explain what they'll need from the other SMEs in the room. Will legal need special reports from the SMEs in accounting? Will the engineering SME need to collaborate with the IT SME on a SME database? And so on.

Learn to translate. SMEs speak a language called SME. You may have heard it before; it comes in several dialects: SME_{LEGAL}, SME_{IT}, $SME_{ENGINEERING}$, and more. An example:

You: "What's wrong with the project intranet?"

SME: "There's a TCP/IP stack error and the RAM disk on the Apache server is unstable."

SME in translation: "It's broke."

Remember that a project manager is above all a fine communicator. It's not merely your job to keep the trains running on time; it's your job to ensure the engineer can talk to the fireman and the fireman can talk to the stoker. So part of your job is to translate among SMEs and between SMEs and non-SMEs alike, a tough job indeed. You'll need to learn just enough SME (the language) to speak intelligently with SMEs (the people), and you'll need to become adept at rendering the complex ideas of experts in plain, simple English, or helping them do it themselves.

To that end, remember that a SME who can speak in plain English is a rare find and should be hired as part of your project team immediately.

Never waste a SME. A good lawyer once told us that nearly a third of his clients in his career (which spanned some three decades and took him from the backwoods courts of Louisiana to the Supreme Court no less than twice) hired him and gladly paid his outrageous hourly fee only to ignore his advice. The result? "They got themselves into a lot of trouble," he said.

Remember that SMEs are experts. They've spent years, often decades, learning their craft, and if one thing is true, they tend to know it well. While you can feel free to discard a SME's thoughts on management and project management in particular, discard his advice in his field of expertise at your own peril. In other words, when the lawyers talk law, listen, no matter how much it hurts. If the geeks in IT tell you the database can't handle the number of records you need, no matter how many times you hit the computer, believe them.

Bear in mind that you're paying your SMEs a good deal more than you're paying your other team members. Perhaps the dumbest thing you could do is discard their advice. You'll not only waste your money, you'll waste your time. And in a project, what's more precious than time?

Let SMEs check SMEs. That said, no SME is perfect, and the best ones know this. That's why it's wise to let SMEs check the work of other SMEs for safety and accuracy. In fact, it's a common practice among certain SMEs. Engineers, for example, often pay other engineers (even competing firms) to check their numbers before they turn in a project, just to be sure they've got it right.

Chapter 2

Perfect Planning Makes Perfect

Ah, projects. Perhaps you've heard of the five stages of project initiation? They tend to begin with euphoria—that pleasant rush to the head when a team dives right in and starts to work, no plan in hand. It's a time when no teacup can hold the tempest of pleasant anticipation.

Then all too soon comes disillusionment. Over time a certain but vague awareness of the inevitable sets in, that feeling that something's not right. Things go (too) slowly; things go wrong. (*Is there really this much work? We never expected this.*)

Then comes the search for the guilty, or the blame stage, followed in short order by the abandonment of the project in the defeat stage. Often (all too often, in fact) we search for someone to scapegoat and team members call to fire the uninvolved. Only after this does project planning really begin.

It's sad, but true. Planning is an overlooked art. It's confused all too often with paperwork, which happens, at least in part, because there are so many bad planners out there—men and women who see planning as little more than filling in forms and checking off lists, men and women with a fetish for Microsoft Project. But it's not.

At the heart of planning is learning to look ahead to keep from falling behind, a skill so rare it ranks with clairvoyance in frequency of occurrence. But, we're glad to note, there is good news: Planning can be learned, and in the pages that follow, we've left you a hint or two on the lost art, the lonely art, the lovely art of planning.

Scope It Out

Listen up. This part's important.

The *statement of scope* is a special tool in your arsenal, one of the few indispensable forms for any PM. In it, you define what you will and won't do in a given project. You define, that is, the *project scope*: the boundaries where a project begins and ends.

Why? Because *scope creep* is the largest problem that most projects face. Scope creep refers to the treacherous way in which projects grow, day by day and little by little, beyond the bounds of reason and out of control. And the only hedge you have against it is the statement of scope.

The essence of the scope statement is simple. It tells your sponsor, "This is what I heard you tell me, this is what I plan to do in response, and here's the cost." Look at it like a contract. It's an agreement between you and the brass on what you'll do and what you won't.

As important as the scope statement itself is the process of writing it. It makes you mull over, in depth and detail, the elements of the project one by one. What's more, the statement, once complete, gives your sponsor your interpretation of the work to be done and makes him validate your interpretation of the work. It's a good way to ensure that you see eye to eye, before problems arise.

So what does the scope statement include? A good scope document has these sections:

An overview This is a paragraph or two that states the project as a problem to be solved. If you need to, borrow some language from your project charter (presuming you have one, which you should). It's one more chance to show the sponsor that you understand his needs, and one more chance to make sure that your understanding of the project is the same as his.

Deliverables Here's where you state what you'll do in depth. List and describe every last item you'll deliver as part of the project's scope. For large projects, this section can take pages and pages, and that's fine. It's better to be verbose than to skimp.

Resource needs Describe what you'll need to get the work done. This includes any people, machines, equipment, and the like.

Cost If you don't have an official budget, here's where you'll write one. Be as detailed as possible—it's the best way to prevent disagreements.

Approval Show the statement of scope to your team and your sponsor. Be sure you have their buy-in. If you don't—if, that is, you write the statement on your own, without their input—you'll have something that's not worth the paper it's written on. More than any other document, the statement of scope is the one that your team needs to know—and agree to—implicitly.

The Green Ceiling

Mark R. is more than a VP at a Milwaukee graphic design firm. Not that you'd know it to look at him. Balding and bespectacled, the owner of a gray Volvo (used, no less), Mark rarely speaks above a whisper and writes everything in pencil (the better to erase with). But in his playtime this man who earned his CPA by age 24 likes to roam the globe in search of thrills. He's trekked the minor peaks of the Himalayas (though never Mt. Everest), spent a week last summer on the Great Barrier Reef, and, for this 40th birthday, threw himself from a plane with a parachute he packed himself. This week he plans to hike the cloud forests of Costa Rica, which, as far as vacations go, works out well. His firm's office is being renovated, and the painters will use the time he's gone to paint his office.

Before leaving he speaks with a painter, who asks him what color he'd like his office to be. In a rush to get home and pack, Mark answers simply, "Green."

Two days later, when Mark is lying in his hotel room in San José, he checks his e-mail by BlackBerry. He finds this missive from his assistant:

M.—

Hurry back. Your office is done. You'll be wanting to see it.

—K.

Upon his return Mark enters his office, the tan of the Costa Rican sun still on him, and sees, much to his dismay, that his walls are hunter green and his ceiling is the same, making his office as bright as a crypt. He summons the painter at once.

"What the hell did you do here?" he says, his voice, for once, above a whisper.

"What do you mean? You asked for green."

"I meant *light* green. And why the hell did you paint the ceiling? Everyone knows the ceiling should be left alone."

"Mister," says the painter, huffing himself up, "you're lucky I didn't paint the floor."

There's a simple moral to this story. Never start a project—any project, no matter how simple—without a well-defined statement of scope. And for Pete's sake, be sure to use any means you have—verbal, written, or even graphical—to communicate the scope of the work to be done. Or you might end up working in a crypt.

Finding Your Stress Points

Want some aspirin?

In the introduction, we said that projects are people, and this is true enough. Projects *are* delivered by people, and in a sense, projects *are* the people who deliver them. But projects are also stress. Not merely stressful, but pure, unalloyed stress. It's the nature of working on deadline and part and parcel of working with people whose quirks can at times infuriate you, not to mention the daily grind of getting things done. And projects, in the end, are all about getting things done. Big things. Important things.

But above and beyond the daily stress of every project are certain *stress points*, moments in time that can last days or weeks when the stress the project puts on its people is more than average—so much more, in fact, that it threatens the project with breaking. Consider a concept from the world of structural design. Every metal has an *elastic stress point*, the furthest point you can bend the metal and still expect it to spring back into shape. Past the elastic stress point, it deforms beyond repair. A stress point in a project is similar: It's a moment in time or an event that makes the project bend and, if it's not well planned for, nearly break.

Perhaps it's the planned change of the PM or some other major figure on the staff. Perhaps it's a change in the project's sponsor (this is common during mergers and acquisitions). Perhaps it's merely a crucial milestone in the project itself—for instance, in a software design project, you'll find stress points at the first user testing cycle, at the first rollout, and at the product's release.

How do you plan for stress points? (After all, stress points become non-events with adequate planning.) So, at the beginning of your next project—perhaps as part of an extended project kickoff meeting—assemble your group for a stress-point meeting. Brainstorm. Look to the future and divine all the possible stress points in your project. Rank them by imminence and impact. Then formulate careful plans to deal with each.

Note that dealing with stress points and doing risk management are not one and the same. Risk management deals with risks that *could* happen; stress points deal with problems that *will* happen, without fail—problems you can see and anticipate from the project's start. Therefore, there's no reason not to plan for them in advance. To do otherwise is simply a mark of sloth or—worse—incompetence. (And if there's anything chicken herders are not, it's incompetent.)

Planning the Project Nightmare

As the saying goes, the best laid plans of mice and men will go to hell in a handbasket if you're not too careful. (Well, something like that.) The point is, it pays to plan ahead and plan carefully. And believe it or not, there's value in planning the project nightmare, in planning the many ways a job can go wrong so you know how to make it go right. It's really very simple. The best way to keep a project on the straight and narrow is to know what can derail it, before it has a chance to jump the tracks. Start by getting your team into a single room (if needed, entice them with food). Then brainstorm. This is a risk management exercise, pure and simple. Hence:

- What can go wrong?

- What can harm us?

- What risks are waiting for us?

For instance, is our data center in a hurricane zone? Do our executives travel on the same plane? Is the product we're about to release insufficiently protected by patents? A few minutes into this meeting you'll have a list of risks as long as your arm. And to make it longer, and thus more complete, invite your client's or project sponsor's input. They'll often have a viewpoint that's different from yours.

Now that you've got the risks, quantify them. Assign a dollar amount to each risk on your list by using this simple formula:

Probability of Risk × Economic Impact = Cost of Risk

Let's do one together. Let's say there's a small chance—no more than 10 percent—that a storm will wipe out your data center valued at $5,000,000. The cost of the risk is $500,000, or 10 percent of $5,000,000.

Now, let's say you've got the option of adding storm shutters and raised floors to your data center. They can lessen the damage caused by a storm, or even keep the storm from doing any damage at all, but they cost nearly $40,000. Are they worth it?

The answer is yes. The cost of the cure (the storm shutters and raised floors) is less than the cost of the risk. If the storm shutters and raised floors had cost more than $500,000, the answer, of course, would be no. The cost of the cure would exceed the cost of the risk.

Here's a boilerplate risk or two to stay on the alert for (use them to get your discussion with your team rolling):

- Loss of the client

- Wrath of the project sponsor

- Failure of major systems

- Litigation

- Cost overruns

- Breakdown of the project team

- Infighting between teammates

- Patent delay

- FDA rejection

The Givens: Dealing in Advance with Things You Can't Change

There's an old saw: When you assume something, you make an *ass* out of *u* and *me*.

Fair enough. Assumptions, by their very nature, are risky. Yet we make so many of them as part of our projects. We assume that we'll have the full support of our project sponsors—until they withdraw it. (Or hedge their bets, or do a little CYA.) We assume that we'll have enough money to finish the job—until it runs out. Or we assume we'll have adequate staff to meet all our needs—until we don't. The result? We look like an ass. And worse, our projects suffer. Sometimes they suffer all the way to the grave.

So let's make a few definitions. An *assumption* is something that needs to happen for a project to work, but that's outside the control of the project team. In like manner, *constraints* are things that limit or restrict the project and which the team has no control over. Together, assumptions and constraints are called *givens*.

The problem with givens, and above all assumptions, is not that they're out of our control. After all, so much in life is. And like so much else, we can plan for and around them. The problem with givens is that we don't realize we even have them. We don't realize that we make assumptions that have the power to break our project in two if they're wrong.

So what should you do? First, you need to identify your assumptions, and your team's assumptions as well. As part of the project kickoff meeting, run a quick exercise in which you brainstorm project assumptions with your project team. Build a list and circulate it to sponsors, executives, and team members—in short, anyone and everyone involved with your project. Have them vet every assumption for accuracy. Is it true that you'll have an hour's time on the mainframe daily? Will Johnson be here for two weeks in July, when you need him most? Does the accounting software really build those reports you'll need? Once you discover which assumptions are false, rewrite your project plan to account for the new reality you face.

Do the same with constraints. First, identify them in a team meeting: Are there FDA guidelines you'll have to abide by? Are there legal restrictions on the product you're making? Maybe you only have two Java coders to complete a large portion of your software's code, or you only have $200,000 in the bank (money, after all, is one of the classic constraints for any project).

Once you've pegged down your constraints, endeavor to understand their impact—or potential impact—on your project. Once you do, you may need to rework your project plan a bit to account in advance for things you can't change. Believe us, you'll be safer if you do.

Using (and Abusing) Weekly Status Reports

God, we hate paperwork. Like hair in a drain, it clogs and slows your project, but, for so many reasons, it's simply required for good project management. (If you doubt us, try to get through an audit without it.) The trick, of course, is walking the fine line between too little and too much documentation, knowing when to commit information to paper and knowing when to commit your troops to action.

But there's one piece of paper that we find indispensable: the *weekly status report*. It's a study in simplicity and a hell of a tool to organize and manage your project. It can also be abused through misuse, overuse, or no use at all. But first we'll talk about its proper use.

A definition: The weekly status report is a *one-page* recap, a snapshot of where your project stands that week. Not two pages, not ten. If it can't fit on a single page, it's not a weekly status report. It's a narrative.

Next, a description: In addition to bearing the title, date, and other head matter, the weekly status report is divvied into four sections:

Things we've accomplished this week In this section you write the five or six main points of progress you've checked off your lists this week. Stick to the major points; only record what matters.

Things to accomplish next week List the major tasks that lie in wait. Once again, stick to the major points and note only what matters. This is not the place to write *War and Peace*.

Special resource requirements These needs can be people, equipment, cash, or anything else you'll need in the course of the next week to get the job done.

Immediate problems to be addressed Here's where you'll record any pickles or glitches that need the team's immediate attention.

(For you webheads, you'll find a template for weekly status reports on the book's website: www.herdingchickens.com. Information about accessing the templates in this book can be found in the introduction. There's also a sample of what the template looks like in the Appendix.)

Do the weekly status reports religiously. Make sure they're done and distributed every Monday morning by 10 ~AM Distribute them not only to members of your project team, but to higher-ups as well—executives, project sponsors, and owners.

Why are they useful? Simple. Beyond the obvious (they're a means to record the state of your project once a week for its duration), they're also a means to subtly pressure your project's underperformers to pick up the pace. If, for example, a team member continually lists an item in the section named *Things to accomplish next week,* he's gone on record that his work isn't done. If it stays there for weeks at a time it becomes an embarrassment to him, a constant reminder, once a week at 10 A.M., that he's yet to finish his obligations. (In fact, it's for this very reason that weekly status reports are so damn hard to get done: Project members are loathe to admit they're behind in their work, and as a consequence, they hem and haw or outright refuse to commit their items to the report.)

But there's more to it than that. In building a one-page rundown of your project's status, you've also built a sleek little tool to communicate the state of your work with your firm's executives and upper crust. You can show them what you're doing and what progress you've made. But most importantly, you can show them what problems remain to be addressed—thorny, nasty problems that may need their heft or political weight to be solved. Hence the weekly status report becomes a way to manage your managers.

Archives are the last use for weekly status reports. Take all your reports and bundle them together in a binder; reading them, you'll begin to see trends that you may have missed before. In addition, new team members who hop on board can easily come up to speed on a project's status by taking half an hour to review the archive and see where things stand.

Now, on to the abuse of weekly status reports—and yes, they *can* be abused. How? First, people don't do them. This happens everywhere, because the weekly status report itself becomes a self-reporting tool on what you haven't done but said you would. Team members are skittish to note their sloth on paper.

A second abuse of weekly reports is length—too much of it, to be precise. These should be one-page reports, no more. But there are some (and there are times we feel like we've worked for them all) who feel an utter compulsion to write weekly reports that resemble phone books in size and depth. Please, spare us. A single page will do. Brevity is a blessing.

A third abuse—and a rare one, given its gravity—is the reporting of wrong information. There are, sadly, times when team members simply misreport the facts. They claim they've done things they haven't; they claim they've made progress they didn't. It's a grave error to make. In so doing, they advertise a lie to the entire team and to those executives and sponsors who receive the report. But alas, it happens. And it's your job to protect against it. If you see bogus info in a status report, get out your eraser—fast.

It's also your job to protect against the fourth abuse of weekly status reports: politics. From time to time, status reports can become a political piñata. Team members lash out at one another by noting what hasn't been done but should be, or add to the report cruel or rude comments meant to attack their colleagues. (Example: Mike never got the brochures from Sales; I think he's on crack.) If this happens, it's smart to have a neutral party review the reports before they're sent out. And above all, be sure you have final say over the report before anyone reads it. In fact, you might want to write it yourself. Better safe than sorry.

....

Straight to Video

Christian F. had a problem. A PM with more than a decade's experience in locations as foreign as Lhasa and Abu Dhabi, he was no amateur when it came to running projects overseas. And his linguistic resume was proof of it: Christian spoke Cantonese and Japanese both, and knew, to varying degrees of fluency, smears of Arabic, Tibetan, and Thai. He knew as well how to communicate with the home office, and, as a gifted PM, he knew how to get things done.

But now, tasked with erecting a 30-story glass-and-steel box in Hong Kong, he suddenly found himself unable to get his weekly status reports read by his project sponsors in Boston. Though he sent them weekly like clockwork, he'd invariably receive a call, two or three times a week, from higher-ups asking for updates on the building's status. And those calls were beginning to drain precious time from his schedule.

So he thought at length about his project's executives. These, he realized, were not men who read much or took the time to read much—even the simple faxes he'd been sending them for more than a year. As a result, he'd have to find a new way of communicating the same information in something more, something other than the written word. So Christian turned to video. Each week he taped his status reports and sent the tapes to Boston, where his firm's brass, eager for news, watched them in two or three minutes flat. And as a result, they never called him for updates again.

A picture, as they say, is worth a thousand words.

Stop What You're Doing
(And Start Using Stoplight Charts)

People like pictures. They're worth a thousand words, as they say, and they're easy to digest. So here's one for you to nibble on:

Task/Item	Status
Negotiate contract	🔴
Find contractor	🔴
Appoint project team	⚪
Write scope statement, WBS, project schedule	⚫

⚫ red　　⚪ yellow　　🔴 green

It's called a *stoplight chart*, named, as you can see, for the use of stoplight icons in the right-hand column. (We like to keep it simple here.) And it's easy enough to make. Just use Microsoft Word to build a table with two columns (or use the template found at www.herdingchickens.com. You can see the form in the Appendix). List your open tasks on the left; on the right, assign an icon to each: green for good, yellow for stalled, red for stopped. You can find and copy the icons anywhere on the Web, or, if you're the creative sort, build them yourself in Photoshop or some other graphics app. In fact, you can even use Microsoft Project, the granddaddy of project software, to build stoplight charts on the fly based on your project plan. (Just how to do it is beyond the scope of this book. But you'll find ample directions in Microsoft's help files, on the Web at third-party sites, or at support.Microsoft.com.)

The question, then, is what to use them for, these simple little tools that even a child can understand. The answer? For dealing with management. Stoplight charts are a tool for managing your managers.

How? Just modify them a bit. In the left-hand column, list your project milestones——points of reference that readers (execs, sponsors, and owners) can relate to. These should be major points of progress in the life cycle of your project. In the right-hand column, use the stoplights to fore-cast the chance of completing a milestone by its due date.

Then when you're done, hand the chart off to the higher-ups. The red dots on the chart will draw their attention to problems that need their help. (You can safely expect them to ignore everything in green.)

The stoplight chart is something of an advertisement. It's a way to get an executive's attention, but quick. It's also a way to prep a project sponsor for delays you know are coming down the pike. And it's a way to do it sim-ply and quickly—two words we can never get enough of. And we bet you can't either.

Why Ahead of Time and Under Budget Can Ruin Your Day

Only a twit would deny that a project that's ahead of time is always a coup. Only a dolt would deny that a project that's under budget is always a blessing, a benison. And a project that's *both* ahead of time and under budget…well, that's manna from heaven, right?

Wrong. In fact they're all wrong. They're even stupid. If you're not careful, ahead of time and under budget can ruin your day, for a few simple reasons. Remember, as a PM it's your job to avoid undue surprise, good and bad alike. So if you surprise a project's owner with a project that's under budget (say, by a million bucks), he'll be pleased at first—until he sees he could have put that money to better use if you'd told him about it before, to upgrade a system or to buy some better equipment. True, the project would no longer be under budget—it would be exactly *on* budget—but its quality would be higher. The point is, you need to give the owner the right to decide—after all, it's his money. And one thing we've learned after decades in project management is that owners, unlike children, despise surprises.

The same goes for projects ahead of schedule. Take the issue of warranties, for example. If you install a component six months ahead of schedule—and six months before it can be used—you've wasted six months of warranty, simply because you're ahead of time. Way to go.

Then, of course, there's the time cost of money to consider. In an ideal world you'd like to start every task as late as possible, because every task costs money and you're either earning interest or paying interest on your money. Why spend those dollars today when you can delay them by 30 days down the road?

And if you don't use up all the money you're allotted for a project, you may find it won't come back to you in the next round of budget revisions. For instance, if the sales team in a large company fails to spend every penny of their million-dollar budget for 2005, they may find their 2006 budget reduced by the amount they failed to spend.

So, to avoid the ahead-of-time and under-budget crunch, you need to stay on top of your project budget, updating it monthly, if not weekly (and for some projects with complex budgets, daily). Every month (or week or day) you'll re-estimate your *cost-to-complete*, the amount of money it takes to complete your project. And with that figure in mind you'll know exactly where you stand. You can also keep tabs of every *purchase order (PO)* you sign, so you know exactly what you've committed to in terms of dollars. And you can make nice with your project accountant. He's one of the key subject matter experts (SMEs) on your team, so it pays (literally) to make him a friend.

Inside the Responsibilities Matrix

At the start of a project, confusion and entropy can reign. Team members are new, tasks and even goals are ill-defined, and who does what (the perennial question) is still very much up in the air.

Besides Valium, what you need is a tool to map out team members' responsibilities. Not only will this tool show, with some degree of precision, who does what, but in so doing, it will cut down on internal squabbles and save you valuable time and peace of mind.

Enter the *responsibilities matrix*. It's a chart that shows who's responsible for every task in a project. In a small project, this can be a simple chart—one person writes a document, one person approves it, and another person carries out its instructions. But in a large project, the kind you're apt to be involved in, the responsibility for a single task often lies with several people all at once, hence the need for a chart to clarify the issue.

Take a gander at the chart below:

Activity	Sponsor	Project Manager	Steering Committee	Finance	Legal
Project Charter	I	C	A		
Communications Plan	A	C		I	I
Meeting Schedule	A	C			
Job Cost Reports	R	I		C	
Contracts		I		I	C
Scope Changes	A	C		I	I

It's a simple responsibilities matrix. (You'll find a copy of it at www .herdingchickens.com.) On this matrix, the people in your project are listed as columns from left to right—the sponsor, PM, the steering committee, and so on. Deliverables are listed as rows from top to bottom—Project Charter, Statement of Scope, Communications Plan, and the like. The resulting cells are filled with codes (here, I, A, R, and C) that show who's responsible for what.

Below are some codes you can load into your responsibilities matrix. Feel free to create your own and tailor them to your project team:

- A—Approves the deliverable

- R—Reviews the deliverable

- C—Creates the deliverable

- I—Gives input on the deliverable

- N—Is notified when a deliverable is complete

- M—Manages the deliverable (this would include librarians and others responsible for the document library)

In the preceding matrix, the *Project Charter*, the blueprint for the project, is written by the project manager with input from the project sponsor, approved by the steering committee, and reviewed by the project team. Scope changes, on the other hand, are created by the PM, with input from finance and legal, and approved by the project sponsor.

The value of the responsibilities matrix is not simply in the document itself (although, we admit, it's a useful tool to have around, a simple chart to review at a glance and see who does what in your project), but in the process that lies behind it. In building it you'll be forced to analyze the scope of work and how your team members—not to mention the project sponsors, owners, steering committee, and company executives—relate to that work. It will help you create a fair breakdown of labor. It will let you assign the right people to the right jobs from the start.

Remember to circulate the responsibilities matrix after it's done for approval. Be sure that everyone whose name is on it understands what he's responsible for—now, before the work of the project begins in earnest. Have your team members, your sponsor, and your owners sign off on the document and store those copies in a safe place later. You may need them when disputes arise.

The SWOT Analysis

This one's simple:

Strengths

Weaknesses

Opportunities

Threats

SWOT analyses are basic strategic planning tools you can use at the start of your project to scan the environment for strengths, weaknesses, opportunities, and threats. Strengths and weaknesses are most often internal to your firm; opportunities and threats, external.

For example, some of your strengths may be a crackerjack team with special skills (a knowledge of Armenian business law—always useful—or Visual C++), a strong patent hedge for your products, a good brand name, or a rock-solid distribution network. And your weaknesses? Perhaps a lack of name recognition, a poor reputation among customers, or low margins.

To learn your strengths, ask yourself a few simple questions:

- What do we do well?

- What advantages do we have?

- What knowledge do we bring to bear that others don't?

And for Pete's sake, don't be modest. Now's the time to strut your stuff a bit and throw out your chest. As for your weaknesses, ask yourself these questions:

- What do we do badly?

- What can we improve?

- What should we avoid?

Don't lie to yourself. Now's the time to admit any faults you have. After all, it's best to know them now, when you can minimize and master them, rather than later, when they can bite you from behind.

Opportunities and threats are often outside the firm. Opportunities can include the advent of a new technology, a change in federal regulations, or the bankruptcy of a competing firm. Threats, on the other hand, can include a new competitor on the horizon or a new technology that threatens to make yours obsolete.

Why bother with a SWOT analysis? After all, strategies, tactics, gambits…these are management's duties, no? They barely apply to you, the PM, whose job is to get things done, and surely they don't apply to the members of your team, lower, by and large, on the food chain.

But that's provincial, shuttered thinking. The better you and your team understand the larger environment of your project, the better the work you do. Spending a half an hour on a SWOT analysis as part of a kickoff meeting can pay unseen but tangible dividends down the road. That's time well spent.

WAGs and SWAGs: Range Estimates Are Better

Try to answer these questions:

- What's the budget for a new airport terminal in Salt Lake City?

- How much will it cost to build a new gigabit WAN with SAN backup for your southeastern sales team?

- Your transmission tower in San Diego just blew down. How quickly can you replace it?

Not sure? Take a guess. If you have to, take a *Wild-Assed Guess (WAG)*. If you really have to, take a *Swinging Wild-Assed Guess (SWAG)*. Sometimes there's no other way to make an estimate.

Or is there? God knows there are enough defective estimates in the world. In fact, it can be argued that most estimates are defective in one way or another: They're either too high or too low when compared to the reality of your project. Most estimates are too low. But even the ones that are too high can damage a project. If you overestimate the cost of a project component—be it a piece of equipment or labor or anything else—that's unused money you allocate to the component that could have been used elsewhere, and to good purpose.

The question is, how do you make an estimate that's right on target? WAGs and SWAGs, after all, just won't cut it.

Neither will the traditional way of doing estimates, in which you assign a single number (and not a range) to each project component, then total the numbers to arrive at your project estimate to which you can add a healthy contingency factor, say 20 percent. The simple fact of the matter is that conventional techniques for making estimates aren't cut out to deal with real-world problems.

But *range estimates* are. In a range estimate you specify the lowest and highest values for each element of your project, not merely the single value. How? Let's say you're building a bridge, and you have to estimate the cost of steel as part of your project budget. Based on the current price of steel and your knowledge of how much you need, you estimate that you'll pay $1,000,000 to have the steel delivered to your doorstep. But you know that number could fluctuate down by 2 percent or up by 10 percent, depending on market conditions, timing, and other factors. So your range estimate for steel is $980,000 to $1,100,000. You repeat this for every element in your project to come up with a total range estimate for the project itself.

Item	Budget Amount	Possible % Under	Possible % Over	Low Range	High Range
Foundation	$350,000	0%	5%	$350,000	$367,500
Steel	$1,000,000	2%	10%	$980,000	$1,100,000
Roof	$265,000	5%	5%	$251,750	$278,250
Finishes	$475,000	25%	25%	$356,250	$593,750
Furniture	$280,000	5%	0%	$266,000	$280,000
Total	$2,370,000			$2,204,000	$2,619,500
Budget	**$2,370,000**				
			Possible Underrun	$166,000	
			Possible Overrun		$249,500

You can also use range estimates to give your project sponsors a certain level of input and thus comfort with your budget. For instance, using the steel example above, you ranged your estimate down by 2 percent and up by 10 percent. If that's cutting it close—and if your sponsors agree—you can range the estimate down by 3 percent and up by 12 percent, or down by 4 percent and up by 15 percent, and so on.

If the notion of making a range estimate for every element in your project is daunting, consider the fact of *Pareto's Law*, also known as the *80/20 rule*. It states that a relatively small number of elements in a population will collectively account for a very large percentage of the overall measure of the population. That's a fancy way of saying that 20 percent of

anything will account for 80 percent of the results. Applied to range estimates, 20 percent of your project elements will account for 80 percent of
your budget. So, if you don't have time to range-estimate *every* element of
your project, only range-estimate the 20 percent that accounts for 80 percent of the project's total budget. With the rest, you can simply flat-estimate
their amount and still have a certain margin of safety.

Mapping the Mind

Divide the square root of six by the square of five by the square root of four.

Just kidding. The real test is much simpler and much, much more telling.

Take out a sheet of paper and write out directions to your house. Pretend that you've invited someone to dinner—someone from out of town, say, a friend from college—and you plan to give him directions on a sheet of paper so he won't lose his way. You have *carte blanche* to give the directions as you please, using whatever method or style you find most useful to keep your friend on the right track.

When you're done, turn the page. Like good Willie Shakespeare said, we promise you there's method to our madness.

What did you do? Did you write the directions down as a list, a neat, step-by-step narration of his journey ("Turn left as you exit the hotel and turn right onto I-95; take I-95 to exit 64 and head east…")? Or did you draw a map, a quick sketch of the city with his route through it darkened in pencil? Of course, you may have done both, the better to help him make it on time. Believe it or not, it matters.

If you wrote out a list, you tend to think in strict logical terms. A psychologist might say you have a linear psyche—otherwise put, it moves from point to point in a clean, ordered manner, teleologically. (That hefty little word comes from the ancient Greek word *telos*, meaning goal. List-makers, as you can imagine, are highly results-oriented.) This is very much a left-brain response to the world.

On the other hand, if you drew a map, you tend to think in visual, spatial terms. You see the relationships between items and how they fit together, which is always a plus for a project manager charged with making the trains run on time. You're intuitive and good at getting the big picture, though you may not have the best eye for detail in the world. (Look at your map. It contains only the main streets and arteries, doesn't it?) You're very much a right-brain thinker.

If you did both the list and the map, then kudos. You're a bit of a blend between the two, with a talent for detail but an eye for the big picture as well. You think in logical, linear terms (check your Day Runner and tell us how many lists you've made in the last month or two), but you see the connections between tasks and projects as well. Whether or not you're a right- or a left-brain thinker is anyone's guess, to be determined by other work, thought, and linguistic patterns.

Now consider this. In planning projects, we can make lists (method one in the map directions example) or draw charts (method two). Schedules or Gantts. Statements of scope or work breakdown structures (WBSs). But wouldn't it be nice if we could do both at once, if there were something, some kind of tool, to wrap it all up in a neat little package? Something to give us a nitty-gritty view of the details at the same time that it gives us an insider's view of how they relate to one another?

There is. There has been for 30 years.

But first, a detour into the brain. This organ of Antaean complexity is composed of trillions of cells called *neurons*, the very ones that carry the chemicals responsible for all our thoughts, emotions, feelings, and memories, and the very root of our creativity. We'll spare you a long and boring description of neurons (God knows that more ink has been spilled on the subject than nearly any other), and simply draw your attention to their shape:

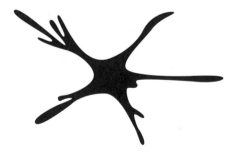

Do you see the central nucleus and the axons that radiate out from it? Good. Keep them in mind, because you're about to learn a new way to plan, think, and organize based on the very way your brain is built to carry out those functions themselves.

In the late 1960s, a man named Tony Buzan invented the *mind map*, a graphic technique to unlock the power of the brain. (Bear in mind that research claims that humans use less than 1 percent of the power of the brain, so any technique that improves on that number is welcome.) Mind maps marshal the full range of cortical skills—word, image, number, logic, rhythm, color, and spatial awareness—in a single, uniquely powerful way that helps you plan and organize like gangbusters. How? Just like neurons work, of course.

Let's say you have a website to build (say, the website for this book, *Herding Chickens*), and you're still in the planning stage. It's a fairly large site, and you need to organize its content—that is, to define the project's scope. You could make a list—which could be several pages long and not very useful since you'd have to flip through pages and pages of data to get a sense of the project as a whole—or you could write a formal statement of scope, which is highly useful but a bit time-consuming. So what's the alternative? You could build a mind map, which lets you see the entire project at a glance. Start by drawing a nucleus in the center of piece of paper; it contains your central idea or theme. Here, it's called "Website Content." (All of the images are pulled from the MindManager program which you can learn more about on their website at www.mindjet.com.)

Website Content

Now draw your first branch (or axon, to keep up the neuron metaphor) out from the nucleus and label it with your first major idea. In this example, you'll use it to mark your first content category:

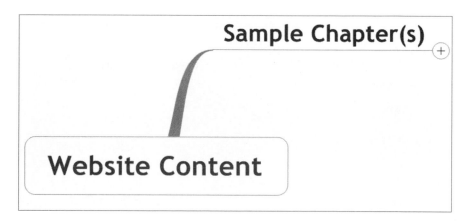

Next, flesh it out with sub-branches to add detail and levels of specificity:

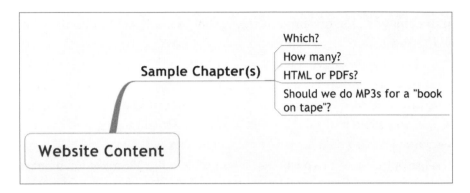

When you're done, add another branch and flesh it out with more detail, and so on and so on, until you've drained your brain of all your ideas. You'll find that your mind map grows like a weed on the page and starts to look something like this:

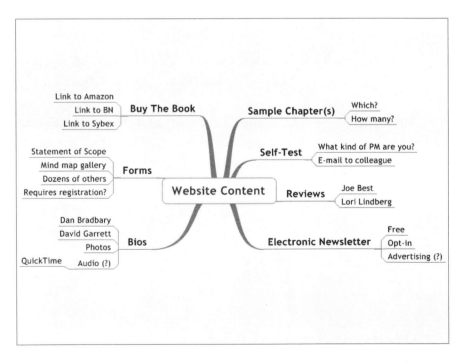

Now step back and think for a second. Do you notice anything? Unlike a list (which is merely linear) or a chart (which is merely visual), the mind map gives you a complete view of the project, namely, one's that's linear and visual all at once. In a single image it shows you structure and details, doing what mere lists or charts simply can't. It gathers and holds large amounts of data in a clean, graphic container that's far more useful than most of the project-planning tools we've been raised to revere (and produce with the mindless fervor of automatons).

The end result? A planning process whose efficiency is improved by orders and orders of magnitude.

Now that you know how they work, why they work, and how to make them, what can you use mind maps for? The answer, of course, is nearly everything, including work breakdown structures like this one:

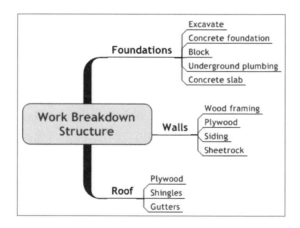

And you won't be alone. Some of the smartest, most intuitive, most creative minds in the world are using mind maps to manage their projects. Here's some proof:

- John Hume, winner of the 1998 Nobel Peace Prize, is using mind mapping in an attempt to solve the Arab-Israeli conflict.

- Myron Scholes, 1997 winner of the Nobel Prize for Economics and professor at Stanford, won't make a presentation with anything *but* a mind map, because it makes his ideas easier to "see."

- Mr. Matthews at the Samuel P. Gompers Vo-Tech High School in New York shows his students how to use mind maps to practice for the U.S. Memory Olympics. The results? So good that Secretary of Education Ron Paige has made several trips to the school.

- Walter Cornell, the president of the firm Up and Running, takes advantage of mind maps for a classic project management purpose: to manage the installation of very large machinery projects for the plastics industry. Of course there's a trick. Cornell is dyslexic, and the visio-spatial nature of the maps and their unique ability to combine the big picture with all its minute details helps him to organize projects with all their multiple restraints, tasks, deadlines, and resources. How many other project management tools can claim to help people conquer dyslexia?

- Shartrina Amato is an educational consultant in Chicago who's used mind maps with children with neuro-cognitive disorders to address their issues with ADD, English fluency, text anxiety, time management, and goal setting.

With uses as wide and varied, as brilliant and eccentric as these, surely there's a place for mind mapping in your project management practice. (Our thanks to MindJet software at www.mindjet.com for sharing these examples.)

The Rolling Wave

"To hell with all this planning. Let's get to work."

Ever heard that before? If you have, there's a good chance you're wearing your team down with too much detail in your project plans. After all, your plans should be sleek and useful; if they resemble a phone book, they're a bit too long. (Don't laugh. We've seen plans that could be used as doorstops, as ballast.)

Consider this: The wrong level of detail can be a gross impediment to your success. If your plans are too detailed, they'll be large and bulky, and they'll chew up all kinds of time just in maintenance alone. If they're too broad, too shallow, or lack enough detail, they'll be as useful to the project team and its sponsors as a skateboard is to a fish.

Far and away the more common problem is to err on the side of detail. Overly detailed plans of the phone book variety require vast amounts of time and money to update, maintain, and change. They chew through paper like termites. And they cause PMs and other managers to spend more time with the plan than they do with their people—always a hazard.

On the flip side of the coin are plans that are overly broad. In these light and flimsy plans, relationships and dependencies are lost, manpower planning and forecasting are impossible, and delays in crucial activities are never recognized in time.

So how do you achieve balance and find the right level of detail in your plans? One way is to use the *rolling wave*. It's simple: Plan your near-term events and activities (those within two–three months) in a sharp level of detail, and leave your long-term events (those more than three months out) in less detail. Then, month by month, roll the wave forward, adding detail to months that were previously left shallow.

Using the rolling wave prevents you from having to manage a huge amount of information throughout the project. Instead, you deal with it as you need it, in waves of detail two to three months out from the present day.

. . . .

The Precisionist

Rena B. had a precision fixation. When she wrote on typing paper, she used a ruler to line the page so her writing would never slant up or down. Her office was immaculate, with nary an out-of-place pen on her desk, and she kept her schedule down to the minute in Microsoft Outlook, her Palm Pilot, and a date planner. (Triplicate, she argued to herself, was safer.)

She knew her exact commute time from door to desk and often spoke in terms of ETAs. She took her coffee with two-and-a-half sugars, never more, never less, and never any cream, since it was too hard to measure. And she regimented her young son's life (school's out at three; piano practice till four; homework from four till six; shower; dinner; a half an hour for TV, then bed) with all the ardor and verve of a bulldog drill sergeant.

She was also a hell of a PM, though she'd only been doing the job for three or four years. But recently she'd run into problems with her project schedule. It was simply too long, nearly a book in length, and she was spending most of her time updating it. Confused, she addressed herself to a senior PM in her firm.

"There's got to be more than this," she said. "I'm spending all of my time on my project schedule. I rarely get to talk with my team anymore."

"Show me the schedule," said the senior PM, a man named Dan who'd spent the better part of his professional life in project management and had the gray hair to prove it.

When Rena unveiled a three-inch binder with a schedule that ran to 100 pages, Dan nearly gasped. "What's in this?" he said, and took the binder to begin reading through its bulk. In less than a minute he'd found the problem. "Look at this," he said. "Look at this entry for your weekly status reports."

"So?"

"It's too long. You could make do with 'Write and distribute a weekly status report.' Instead, you've got 'Write and distribute a weekly status report' followed by one, two, three, four, five …seven subtasks: 'Solicit data from team leaders,' 'Type report in Microsoft Word,' 'Run spell check,' 'Print report,' 'Give report to team leaders,' 'Give report to all team members,' and 'Follow-up with e-mail.' Why do you need all that detail?"

"Because that's what's involved in writing the report."

"Sure it is," said Dan, "but you don't need to say it, for Pete's sake. You already know it. So does everyone who reads the schedule. And what's more, you've fleshed out the entire schedule eighteen months in advance."

By now Rena was flustered. "Well, what else am I supposed to do? I can't leave it incomplete!"

"You *can* leave it incomplete. You can fill in a month or two at a time in high detail, as much as you need, then leave the rest sketched out to fill in later."

"Then when do I fill it in?" she said.

"As you need it. You roll the detail forward every month. That way you don't spend all the time in the world on the damn schedule. You'll have more time for your team."

She looked at him long and hard, knowing, though she'd never admit it, that he was right. 🖎

Chapter 3

Tips Not Typically Taught

There's an old adage: Law school is not lawyers' school. Otherwise put, it teaches you very little about the real-world practice of law. What it does, as you'll learn if you ask any lawyer, is teach you a good deal about the theory of law and how to think logically. But you won't find a course on dealing with clients, and you won't be taught the finer points of cross-examination. Lawyers have to learn those tricks by doing them.

Luckily, training for project managers is a bit more pragmatic. You'll learn how to manage risks and write a statement of scope, how to set goals and hit them. But you won't learn *all* the skills you'll need to be a fine project manager, like how to read people, how to speak well, and how to conduct a post mortem.

So we'll teach you a few of these skills in this chapter.

Reading People

Let's say, for the sake of argument, you ask me if that meeting with our new client went well. "Absolutely," I tell you—but as I speak, my Adam's apple bobs ever so slightly up. Am I lying?

Most likely, as anyone versed in the art of reading people can tell you. During speech, vertical movement of the Adam's apple (also known as the cartilage on the larynx, or voice box) indicates doubt, indecision, and even deceit. It's one of the simplest cues of our *body language*, the gestures and facial expressions we use to speak without words. And it's a useful trick to know if you're a project manager.

Why? To manage projects you have to manage people, since it's people who get your projects done. And sadly, people don't always tell the truth, which is why a good knowledge of body language is essential for good project managers.

Of course, there's more to it than just detecting lies. If you know how to read your team members' body language, you can better grasp their moods and needs, have true dialogues, and even run better team meetings. What's more, you can pay attention to your own body language to be sure you're not sending any signals you don't mean to.

Below we've assembled some concepts on the fine art of reading people by reading their body language (as seen in *The Nonverbal Dictionary* by David Givens):

> **Angular distance** This term refers to the angle of our shoulders in relation to another person. Without knowing it, we often aim our shoulders towards people we like or merely agree with; we turn our shoulders away from those we dislike or disagree with. Richard Nixon was known to show his displeasure with an aide's performance with a pronounced angular distance. During meetings and briefings, he would turn away from those he disagreed with, even as he voiced agreement with their positions. As a PM, you should pay close attention to project team members in meetings. They may tell you they agree with you—after all, as the PM, you're in charge—but veer their shoulders away as they say it.

Arm cross Across the globe, crossed arms are a sign of perceived attack, so be on the watch for team members who take this defensive stance with you or another member of your project team. Studies of college-age American women have shown that women tend to cross their arms before men they dislike, but use open-arm positions when speaking with men they relate to.

You might discover that you have an antagonizing team member if he or she inspires this stance in others in your group. In that case, think long and hard about pairing him with others for special projects.

Bend away Anthropologists have long known that we position our upper body in ways that unwittingly show our emotional response to a speaker. Bending away from a speaker—whether right, left, or back—reveals shock, anger, or extreme dislike.

Watch for this stance when you're talking with accountants and making budget requests. If they lean back as you throw out some numbers, you know you're on thin ice.

Blank face An emotionless face in which the muscles are neither stretched nor contracted, the blank face sends a strong "Do Not Disturb" message. In elevators, in subways, or in any crowded space, we put on a blank face to distance ourselves from those around us.

If you meet your boss in the elevator and his face is blank, do no more than say hello. It's not a good time to talk about your project; instead, make an appointment to see him in his office, when he'll be more receptive to your thoughts.

Broadside display This term refers to the act of enlarging the body's size to threaten or bluff a speaker, most often an opponent. It stems from an ancient reflex: Humans and other vertebrates have always tried to seem bigger to show dominance over their opponents. So if your boss puffs out his chest and squares his shoulders to you, watch out: You're in for a lashing.

In the office, men will often do this to women as a means of intimidation. (Of course, any man who feels the need to intimidate a woman shows that he's the one, on some unconscious level, who's truly threatened. If you're a female PM and a male team member gives you a broadside display, just stand your ground, look him firmly in the eyes, and don't back down. Remember that at base, people—and animals, too—only make this movement when they're frightened or need to bluff an opponent.)

Chin jut When you tilt your head back and stare down your nose, thus jutting out your chin, you show arrogance and disdain towards your speaker. If anything, this is a simple sign of perceived superiority.

Subject matter experts (SMEs) often do this when they're asked to explain a technical point of their discipline. Don't let it get to you, and don't let it get to your team members either. If, by the way, you find a SME who can explain her discipline in clear terms without condescension, hold on to her for dear life. This kind of SME is worth her weight in gold.

CLEM CLEM stands for conjugate lateral eye movement, a movement in which your eyes unwittingly glance left or right without your conscious control. It signals doubt or information processing, and it can signal a lie when combined with a pause in conversation. In a classic study of mathematicians, it was noted that eyes moving right marked symbolic or logical thinking, while eyes moving left marked visual or creative thinking.

When you ask a team member where his overdue work is and his eyes undergo CLEM, you know you're being snowed.

Cutoff This term refers to a motion in which the head is turned fully to one side (right or left, no matter) and the gaze of another person entirely avoided. In conversations, a sudden cutoff signals doubt or the desire to end a conversation.

Got a talker in your group? Someone who can't shut up? Use the body cues that tell him to stop so you can get on with your day.

Eye contact Direct eye contact can arouse strong emotions between speakers. It rarely lasts more than a few seconds (three at the most) before one or both speakers avert their eyes. Studies show that sustained, direct eye contact can raise stress levels (as measured by breathing and heart rate). The lack of direct eye contact can indicate dishonesty, doubt, or frustration.

Not all projects work out, and in your career you're bound to have some failures. When you do, you'll have to explain it to your boss. Look him directly in the eye and state what went wrong—even if he's the problem. Sometimes you have to speak truth to power.

Eyebrow-lower When you knit, wrinkle, or pucker the brow by contracting the corrugator, procerus, and orbicularis oculi muscles, you show disagreement, doubt, or uncertainty.

Watch your sponsor's brows the next time you show her a statement of scope. If they move down as she reads, it's a telling sign of disagreement, and disagreements in scope can sink a project before it even begins.

Eyebrow-raise When you raise the brows, you accentuate your current emotion, whether it's doubt, anger, rage, disbelief, or joy. And who can forget the extreme expression of doubt that's made by raising only one eyebrow at a time?

The best PMs run meetings well. This means knowing when to shut down a team member who's pushing his own agenda. In this case, a single raised brow can do more than a thousand words to show your distaste.

Flashbulb eyes When the superior and inferior tarsal muscles widen our eyes to make them appear larger, rounder, and whiter, it's a sure sign of surprise, terror, or rage. In someone who's angry, it's a sign of imminent physical or verbal attack.

True, you can widen your eyes and feign the appearance of surprise or anger, but real flashbulb eyes are nearly impossible to fake. Because it's so extreme, it's rare that you'll see this nonverbal cue in the office, but when you do, tread with caution. You're dealing with someone on the edge.

Flexion withdrawal For anthropologists, this term refers to a reflexive body movement, an escape motion in which a part of the body is removed from immediate danger. In business, colleagues around a conference table may show their silent emotions of dislike, disagreement, or disdain by pulling their arms off the table or flexing back in their chairs.

If you'd like to encourage a timid team member to share his thoughts, lean forward in your chair as he speaks. (And don't make too much direct eye contact; it can make him nervous.)

Gaze down Watch out: When a speaker points his eyes towards the floor, he may be lying. (True statements are often voiced with a confident eye-to-eye stare.) He may also be feeling guilt, doubt, or simply defeat.

Project sponsors don't always tell the truth, nor for that matter do executives, certainly where budgets are concerned (since budgets, we know, are often a matter of politics). If your project has run out of money and you've been promised a quick infusion of cash, pay close attention to the person who's promised it to you. Did he look you straight in the eye and tell your salvation is coming, or did he hem and haw and gaze towards the floor as he told you, "We'll do the best we can to help"?

Head-tilt-side While a head tilted on its side has a bevy of meanings (in romantic interludes, for instance, it can indicate coyness, even submission), in business it tends to indicate deference.

How do you address your boss? Some executives—mostly the egomaniacs—like to see their underlings show signs of submission when speaking. Others—the sane ones (and hence the rare ones)—prefer an equal and open rapport. Do you talk to your boss with a straight spine and a calm gaze, or do you tilt your head and hedge your words?

Lip compression When the lips are pressed together into a thin line, it's a sure signal of anger, grief, or uncertainty. Slight lip compression can signal opposition or disagreement between speakers.

Watch for this signal in meetings or three-way conversations. When team members tense their lips in reaction to another team member's thoughts, you know they object, no matter what comes out of their mouth.

Steeple gesture This is a hand position in which the fingertips of one hand gently touch the fingertips of the other, forming a steeple. It tends to indicate careful thought. At a conference table a hand steeple can mean that a speaker is paying special care to his words or listening thoughtfully to a colleague's.

If, during a meeting, a team member or sponsor who's about to speak makes the steeple gesture and remains quiet, don't interrupt (or let anyone else interrupt, either). Chances are, you're about to hear a well-thought-out proposition.

Zygomatic smile This is a true smile, one in which the corners of the mouth curve upward and the corners of the eye crinkle into crows-feet. (It's named for the zygomaticus muscle that controls these actions.) By implication, then, other smiles are suspect. (Take the polite smile, for instance, in which the risorius muscles pull the corners of the lips sideways.)

Part of your job as a PM is to be the team's cheerleader-in-chief, not just its leader. So give credit where credit is due, and on occasion, give praise when someone deserves it—but give it with an open smile, holding nothing back. With honest praise there's no room for half-measures. Besides, people always know the real thing when they see it.

Now, a word of caution: Reading body language is fine and good, but you need to read *all* the parts of a person's communication to know his full intent—his body language, his speech, even his clothes. If not, you only get half the picture, and that can be worse than none at all.

A Tip or Two on How to Talk

To manage a project—correction: to manage a project *well*—you need the respect of your colleagues. Frankly, it can make or break your project. And more than anything else, more than how you dress or how you look, how you speak determines how people judge you, how they react to you, and how you're perceived. To put it another way, the better you speak, the better you can manage people, and hence, the better you can manage projects. And we're not talking about the fine (and daunting) art of public speaking, which horrifies most people by nature. We're talking about the simple day-to-day interactions you have with your colleagues on your project team and the executives and sponsors you have to finesse.

Yet for all this, few of us are trained to speak well. Apart from a high school debate class, what formal training do we get in the lost art of conversation—or even better, the art of presentation? (How many presentations have you given in the last six months? How many were you trained for?)

Even linguists, as a whole, tend to ignore this subject. The fields that touch on the nexus between speech and power—discourse analysis, stylistics, and sociolinguistics—are the most fully marginalized in the discipline.

Sadly, no book can teach you how to speak well. And this book is no exception. In this world of e-mail and the World Wide Web—both of which, we'll note, are inherently written media—good speech is a dying art that takes years of practice and a slew of good teachers to master. But we can give you a tip or two on how to talk, the better to manage your colleagues and projects alike:

> **Avoid the appearance of lying.** As you saw in the last section, shifting your eyes left or right—and especially left—while speaking or gazing down can alert your listeners that you're telling a fib. So can any fidgeting on your part. So don't scratch that itch on your arm or run your hands through your hair. Don't straighten your tie or fix your pleats. Just say what you need to say—simply and directly. In other words, look your listeners in the eye and let it rip.
>
> Talk straight with your project team. When you've got bad news to deliver, look them right in the eyes and be honest. Remember, they look

to you, as the PM, for most of their information. You're the source, and you've got to be reliable. Above all, good communication is a matter of trust.

Get good at small talk. It may seem useless to you, but it's an art you need to master, and it's damn hard. The first rule of chitchat is to match the mood of your speaker. If he's in a good mood, ask him why. If he's in a bad mood, empathize. Find a way in and get him to talk. It's easier than having to talk yourself.

With a little charm, you can loosen up your sponsor (maybe he'll budget more funding for your project) or a team member (maybe she'll take on that extra work and get the job done faster).

Learn sociolects. Every social group has its own dialect; they're called sociolects. Your engineers have one. Your eggheads have one. Every SME you've ever met has one. So learn them and start to use them. If you can speak to people in their own terms, in words they're used to, you're ahead of the game already.

Take the time to read some books or websites in many SME disciplines. You don't need to become an expert in their technical fields, but you should get a good handle on the basic vocabulary that's used by accountants, lawyers, coders, and so on. If you do, they'll warm to you; they'll think you're batting for their team—and that's invaluable during a high-stress project.

Never joke at another's expense. It seems like a simple rule, the kind that people would follow. But you'd be surprised to learn how much we tease each other in the name of good-natured fun. The truth is, it rarely works. People take offense, even if they don't let you know. And there's nothing worse than someone who hates you but won't say it. So when a joke comes to mind that could hurt someone's feelings, button it up. You'll be glad you did in the long run.

Most teams have a joker, a person who's too caustic for his own good. His comments do nothing but tick others off, and in the end that hurts team unity. If you've got a joker in your court, take him aside and explain the effects of his comments. Make sure he gets it, too, and work to reintegrate him into the team.

Share the sentiments of the receiver. This one's easy. If you have to deliver bad news, do it with a measure of compassion. If you get to deliver good news, give it with a measure of delight, and not the reverse. Don't tell someone they're fired while smiling, and don't tell someone they've won the lotto in a tone of voice that says you're jealous. Do your level best to match your delivery with the news at hand; if you do, you'll build amity, not enmity.

A little empathy goes a long way. So does sincerity. And both are rare in the politically charged atmosphere of the office. No matter how busy you are, how harried you are, or how much you need to leave to get to your next meeting, take some time to put yourself into your team members' shoes. Not only will you earn their respect (and maybe their trust), but you'll understand your team's dynamics with greater precision than any number of management books can give you.

Don't hem and haw. This one's hard. Try to speak without saying "uh" or "and, uh," two common tics. (Most people can't.) Instead, deliver your message directly, without any extra words or pauses. Trust us: It's a skill that takes practice.

It ain't easy to speak to executives. They can be imposing and often forbidding. But they're also the ones who control your budget, so you need to wow them with your awesome verbal ability. When you're first presenting a project for approval and seeking a budget, practice your presentation until you can say it backwards and forwards. Then deliver it to the brass with panache. The better you speak, the more they'll overlook minor flaws in your plan. (Otherwise put, a little eloquence covers a lot of sins.)

Speak in your chest voice. Most of us speak in a high tone of voice—our head voice—that's an octave or two above where it should be. (It's also nasal and tinny.) Our chest voice, by contrast, is lower, deeper, and resonant. It's also more soothing. Research shows that people warm to the lower registers of speech and shy away from speakers whose voice is high and whining.

While it may not seem to, this tip applies to women as well as men, even though women, by nature, tend to speak in a higher register. Research shows that gender aside, we all speak in a higher tone of voice than we could. So, when chairing your next meeting, drop your voice an octave and speak clearly. But whatever you do, be sure to practice it first. You don't, in an unpracticed attempt, want to sound like Darth Vader on codeine. So do this with care; your chest voice takes practice to make it seem natural.

According to David Wallechinsky and Amy Wallace's *The Book of Lists* (Little, Brown & Company, 1993), public speaking is the number one fear of most Americans: in contrast, fear of death and dying ranks seventh. More than 40 percent of all Americans are deathly scared of speaking in front of groups of four or more. Are you? If you are, follow these simple tips to keep your cool:

Know the room. Get familiar with the place where you'll be speaking. Arrive ahead of time and stand at the lectern. Sit in the chairs in the audience. Walk the room and learn its acoustics. If you want to, practice.

Know the audience. Know what they want, what they want to hear, and what they need to hear. If you can, greet them as they enter the room. It's easier to talk to people you know than people you don't.

Know your material. How do you get to Carnegie Hall? Practice, practice, practice. The more you know your stuff, the better you'll speak. If you're unfamiliar with your own material, your audience will know it immediately—and you'll freeze and stutter.

Relax. Breathe deeply. Think of something pleasant. Calm your nerves. If you're at ease you'll put your audience at ease, and you'll deliver one hell of a speech. After all, two of the greatest speakers of our time, Ronald Reagan and Bill Clinton, were utterly relaxed at the podium. True, each had a distinct style (and they rarely if ever agreed), but you've never seen them stutter, stammer, or blush before a crowd. Speaking came to them as simply and easily as breathing.

Dealing with Bean Counters

Accountants are a special breed of people. They live in their own world of debits, credits, and balance sheets, and thrive on precision and decimals. And since money is one of the biggest constraints of any project, you can expect them to review your work with a fine-tooth comb—and you can expect them to find the occasional problem. After all, who among us has never seen a project with a budget that's too optimistic?

Bear in mind that when accountants do this, they're only doing their job. It won't help matters to bitch and moan and play the enemy. Instead, as a good PM, you should partner with your friendly bean counter and learn to speak his language. It won't hurt you to take a course or two in the basics of finance. (In fact, it may even help. A good PM is always looking to expand her skills.) If you treat accountants like any other SME and follow the rules for SMEs outlined in Chapter 1, "Building the Killer Project Team," you'll learn to speak their language, not only to better communicate with them but to be able to translate between accountants and the nontechnical members of your team.

Remember that accountants plan for the long term—not in hours, days, or weeks, but in months, quarters, and years. Why? Because their job has a cyclic schedule. Once a month, the books must be balanced and closed, after which all kinds of reports are issued to show what you've spent on your projects, including labor costs, materials, overhead, and administrative expenses. Much of this data shows up in the *job cost report*, which breaks down the cost incurred by each line item in your budget.

Job cost reports are a fine way for PMs (and bean counters, too) to constantly forecast where they stand with their budgets. They look like this:

Description	Budget	Cost-to-Date	Cost-to-Complete	Total Cost	Variance
Steel	$100,000	$65,000	$43,000	$108,000	<$8,000>
Concrete	$47,000	$49,000	$3,000	$52,000	<$5,000>
Roofing	$27,000	$0	$24,000	$24,000	$3,000
Plumbing	$19,000	$4,000	$12,000	$16,000	$3,000
Electrical	$22,000	$2,000	$20,000	$22,000	$0
TOTAL	$215,000	$120,000	$102,000	$222,000	<$7,000>

The accountants will provide you with the *cost-to-date* (i.e., what you've spent on a line item up till now). It's your job to forecast the *cost-to-complete* as carefully as possible. (The cost-to-complete is the amount of money you expect to spend on a line item in order to complete that item.) This leaves you with the *total cost*, or the cost-to-date plus the cost-to-complete. The *variance* is the amount that your total cost differs from what you budgeted. If the variance is negative $5,000, you're $5,000 over budget. If it's positive $2,200, you're in the black by more than $2,000. The job cost report automatically adds up all of the columns, and the total in the Variance column tells you whether the total project is currently forecast to be over or under budget.

Because job cost reports are combinations of present costs and forecasts, they force you to revisit your project costs every month. And while that's a bit tedious, it's the only way to keep an accurate eye on the overall cost of your project as it unfolds.

Now, bear in mind that bean counters won't give you this information without asking for something in return. They want to know how you're doing on your budget. You see, accountants are like project sponsors: They don't like to be surprised. They want that warm and fuzzy assurance that you won't exceed the monies they've set aside for your project. More so than budget underruns, budget overruns make them very nervous. With the latter, they have to scramble to find extra dollars for your project, possibly at the sake of your buddy's project across the hall (or possibly with that favorite banker who will loan them a few bucks). Hell, they may even ask you to accompany them to the bank, along with your explanation of why you need the money.

Good PMs keep a close eye on the budget to avoid the unpleasant but ever-present threat of surprise. By forecasting the budget monthly, the project scope may be increased or decreased. But this decision should be based upon the input and approval of the project sponsor and the end user.

It's All About Timing

Larry K., despite his doctor's orders (and his wife's pleadings), bought a dozen doughnuts for the weekly Monday meeting at his job site, the construction of a new terminal at the Dayton airport. He was in the middle of a sugar fix when Paul C., the accountant assigned to the project by the airport authority, nudged him on the shoulder. "Larry," he said, "are you ready to go over those numbers with me this morning?"

Larry was none too excited to see him. Who wants to run budgets on Monday morning, the worst time of the week? But Larry knew Paul was a decent guy, even though, at times, he came across as a bean counter. "Sure," he said. "I'll be ready at 10:00."

Larry and Paul had planned to discuss the project's future cash needs. For large projects such as this, the schedule on which funds are released to the project staff is often just as important as the size of the budget itself. Otherwise put, *when* you get the money is just as crucial as how much you get in total. And accountants, working in concert with PMs, need to precisely forecast your cash flow to make life simpler for the guys in finance who raise the money—and dole it out—in the first place.

When Larry sat down with Paul, the PM rolled out his spreadsheets showing the monthly cash flows needed for the budget's more than 300 line items. All of this totaled up to a tidy sum on a monthly basis: in April, $3.5 million; in May, $4.7 million; in June, $8.2 million; and so on.

With numbers in hand, Paul was able to take the projections back to the airport authority and outline exactly what next year's cash needs were. The result? He could request more money from the finance department.

There's a simple lesson to be learned here: Sometimes, it's just as crucial to know when your project needs some cash as it is to know how much money it needs in total.

The Lost Art of the Interview

Interviews? Interviews? What do interviews have to do with good project management?

Just about everything. As a PM, you'll need to interview new team members and job candidates. You'll need to interview SMEs to get their opinions. You'll need to interview sponsors to get their take on a project and what matters to them. (Consider the Pleasure and Displeasure List in Chapter 4. What better way to find out what matters to whom than to do a round of brief interviews?) You'll need to interview team members to do evaluations. And you'll need to interview clients at the outset of projects to help determine scope and deliverables.

In brief, you'll need to do interviews, whether they're five-minute shorts or two-hour affairs, to gather information. And PMs thrive on information: its acquisition, ordering, and dissemination. No device—not books, memos, or hallway chats—is more important to that than the simple interview.

With that in mind you need to know the basics of a good interview. It's an art, if a dying one, that even journalists who live and die by the interview are often ill-prepared for. But it's not hard. Just follow these rules for good results.

Be organized. Ask yourself, "What do I know? What don't I know? What do I need to know?" Never do an interview on the fly unless you utterly have to. Approach each interview with a list of questions in hand and a mind for how to ask them. Remember: Your subjects may not be prepared, but you should be—there's simply no excuse not to be.

Start small and ratchet up. Interviews can be touchy affairs. You may have to conduct an interview to elicit confidential or even damaging information from your source. (For example, *Why did this task go wrong? Who's at fault? Where do we go from here?*) In times like these it helps to start with smaller, less abrasive questions and build your way up to the big ones. Use simple, harmless queries to build a base for the conversation and then ease into the hard stuff once you've established rapport.

Ask and ask again. It's an old trick: Ask the same question at different times in the interview. Each time a source answers, his answer will be slightly different, giving you a different take on the issue and an overall answer that's nuanced with many facets.

Shut up. This is a basic, but vital, rule. Talk as little as you can, and let your source do the talking for you. What's more, don't be afraid to be silent. Linguists have shown that silence is vexing to most speakers. If you're quiet, your source will feel the need to fill the silence with sound, repeating his answers and adding new information as he does. Ironically, if you simply button your lip you'll find you get more information than someone who asks scores of questions.

Be dumb. Don't be afraid to ask basic questions. People love to explain their work and the basics of their craft, and they'll rarely deem you stupid for asking a basic question in as simple and direct a manner as possible. (In fact, they may appreciate your doing so.)

Romancing Clients

Ah, Clients. They bitch and moan. They complain. They pester. They ask for the world and expect you to give it—twice, often ahead of schedule and under budget. And they have every right to. After all, that's what they pay you for.

As PMs, not all of us have the luxury of working in-house in a company large enough to afford the cutting edge of project management. Some of us—indeed, a large minority—work as freelance PMs or consultants. We have all the headaches of "normal" PMs—the deadlines, stress, and pressure—and the morass of client management as well.

So what's a body to do? Start with the tips below. They're not an exhaustive list of client management techniques, but they'll keep you on the straight and narrow (and they may even save your sanity).

Promise only what you can deliver. It's tempting to offer the world to clients, especially new ones—and most of them demand it anyway—but you need to manage your client's expectations carefully. Better to underpromise and overdeliver than its reverse. Remember that until you give them a reason not to, clients will take you at your word. So give it carefully.

Acknowledge your errors. Nobody's perfect. Mistakes happen to the best of us, and they'll happen to you, too. In fact, they'll happen when you least need them and can least afford them, and they'll happen with clients who demand nothing less than perfection from you and your team. So be up front and acknowledge your errors. You'll find that clients, even the worst, will forgive a mistake if you own up to it— but they won't forgive arrogance.

Talk. A lot. Keep your lines of communication open, and whatever you do, don't leave clients hanging. You should call and e-mail them frequently to get their input and take their pulse.

Don't surprise 'em. It's genetic: Clients hate to be surprised. They'd sooner dine with Hannibal Lecter on a day pass. As a PM, it's your job to run a project with the sophistication and sleight of hand it takes to eliminate any and every surprise that may come down the pike.

Invest in CRM. *Customer relationship management (CRM)* software can save your life (or at least your business). It's designed to track clients, client communications, referrals, and billing. A simple piece of software like Act! (www.act.com) can organize all of your client information in one interface, track unlimited calls, meetings, and tasks, and manage your sales pipeline with forecasting tools and built-in reports.

Insist on a contract. Or at the very least, a signed letter of understanding. Going to work without one is like playing with fire—sooner or later, you and the client get burned. All too often a good PM with good intentions starts a project without a contract in place, only to see the project dissolve before his eyes with no document to govern who was responsible for what, and why.

Outline the client's responsibilities. God knows they're all too quick to outline yours. Make sure you have a document (whether it's a contract, a letter, or a simple memo) that explicitly tells the client what he's supposed to do to make this engagement work. Beyond paying, what are his responsibilities? Will he give you equipment? People? Advice? If so, make sure he knows it—and make sure you have a written record to boot.

Use a statement of scope. We assume you always do, as a good PM. In fact, if you choose to use no other document from the project management arsenal, choose this one. It's far and away the most important. In the scope statement, you'll outline where the project begins and ends, what you'll do and what you won't. It's essential to avoid scope creep and manage a client's expectations.

Keep your invoicing current. Before, we said that clients hate to be surprised. And the worst way to surprise them is with the bill. Better to invoice in small monthly amounts than to present a client with a whopper of a bill at the project's end. You'll avoid more than sticker shock. You'll avoid the potential coronary as well.

Get your client out of the office. You'll tend to get better, more honest appraisals of where things stand when your client's in a relaxed setting—say, a good restaurant. Every so often, take your client out to eat, and use the opportunity to ask him how the project is going. He'll loosen his reins when he's out of the office, and you'll get better info as a result.

Ask what's wrong. A good client is one who'll tell you what's wrong (and then let you fix it). But good clients are rare, so be sure to ask your clients for their input—even their negative input—as much as you need to. If you do, you'll never be surprised yourself.

Don't Get Burned

Allen L. had been a contract PM for more than 10 years, working for clients as varied as mom-and-pop shops with only a dozen workers to Fortune 100 firms in all their might and majesty. (In fact, he'd done five projects for major airlines, the last with a budget of more than $10,000,000.) Before he earned his PMP in June 1994, he worked as an attorney, so he also knew his way around a contract.

And like most vendors, he'd been burned more than once. He'd seen his share of projects derail when clients failed to meet their obligations, despite the best work—and urgings and pleadings—of skilled PMs. So in recent years he'd taken to writing contracts that not only spelled out his own work and what he'd be paid, but what the client would do as well, and most importantly, when.

For instance, his standard contract, written in clear and simple English to avoid confusion, always contained the following clause:

Client's Duties

In addition to prompt payment as outlined in section 10 below, the Client agrees to:

- Read, sign, and return the Statement of Scope within five business days of receipt. Any changes to the Statement of Scope will be made in writing and initialed by the Client.

- Read, sign, and return the Project Charter within five business days of receipt. Any change to the Project Charter will be made in writing and initialed by the Client.

- Read, complete, and return all RFCs (Requests for Clarification, a sample of which is attached) within two days of receipt.

- Return all calls and e-mail within one business day of receipt. Failure to return a call or e-mail as agreed may alter the Project Schedule at the sole discretion of the Vendor.

For Allen's new project with a major U.S. airline—one he'd bid for more than a month ago and was glad to receive, given the fee—the airline agreed to lend him three workers for the project's duration. Allen, ever the lawyer, was sure to put that in writing:

- The Client agrees to provide the vendor with two programmers fluent in C++ for the duration of the project as outlined in the Project Schedule. These programmers will work onsite at the Vendor's place of business and will be paid solely and wholly by the airline.

- The Client agrees to provide the Vendor with one engineer for the first month of the project as outlined in the Project Schedule. The engineer will hold at least a bachelor's degree from a four-year university and be able to use AutoCAD Mechanical 2005 with expertise.

The end result? When, halfway into the project, the airline balked at lending him a second coder, Allen simply produced his contract and reminded them of their commitment. It was a battle he won with ease.

The Post Mortem

Have you ever done an autopsy? We have—all the time, in fact, on projects we've just completed. It's called the *post mortem*, also known as a session for lessons learned or an end-of-project review. And it's a crucial tool in your toolkit.

What is it, exactly? It's simple: a team session in which you gather your group together to review what backfired—and just as importantly, what went right—with a recently completed project. You should also interview all project stakeholders, such as the sponsor or client, to get your results. (For best results, use the interview techniques described earlier.)

Be sure to use this time wisely. Don't simply identify what went wrong; probe as well for why. Why did it happen? Was it a chronic problem or a one-off? (Chronic problems are especially troubling; they indicate a systemic weakness in your company or team.) What outcome did it jeopardize? What problems did it result in? And so on.

Be sure to include the following in your deliberations:

- The initial effort estimates (in man-hours) and the final effort values (again, in man-hours). If you underestimated, as most of us do, how can you avoid it in the future?

- The initial budget and the final cost. Were you over? Under? Why?

- The initial staffing estimates and the actual staffing profiles. Did you have to hire or fire people?

- The initial milestones and schedules and their final, real values. Where were you off?

- The total number of changes to your project's requirements. How many *RFCs (requests for clarification)* were there? The greater the number, the longer—and more involved—your post mortem will be.

....

Cracking the Code and Closing the Cracks

North of 50, Sean F. was a seasoned PM. In his thirty years in project management Sean had consistently been given responsibility for larger and larger projects. And his sheer talent had earned him some plum assignments.

For the last three months, Sean had been spending day and night at the office of a new software house, wrapping up a project he'd inherited prior to joining the firm. It was a good project, the release of new software that helped Web designers write code, and Sean, by and large, was happy (though he felt that better coffee was called for in the break room).

Then all hell broke loose. A week before release, Sean found a a small piece of code that, when called, caused the software to crash. And not only did it cause the software to crash, it caused the user's system to tank as well.

But there was another, more vexing problem. No one seemed to know who wrote that code, or how it got there. And no one knew how to rewrite it, either: It was simply too advanced for Sean's team.

After a day of scrambling, frenzied e-mails, and harried phone calls to the PM who'd run the project before Sean came on board, he was able to find the contractor who'd written the flawed snippet of code and arrange for its rewrite. Thank God. Had the project's release been delayed by so much as a day, Sean's job—and the jobs of his team—would have been as safe as a chicken on the chopping block. Later, when the storm had passed, Sean began to make inquiries in his new firm, and found that the use of vendors like the one who'd mangled his code was left wholly to the PM in charge of the project. That much was fine, but once the project was done and the team disbanded, no one, Sean learned, had bothered to do a post mortem and save the data for the sake of the next PM who came knocking.

Sean would not let his firm make the same mistake twice. Using this snafu as the first of many initiatives, he set out to establish a formal close-out process for each project he chaired. It not only kept data from the close-out meeting, but organized all the project's documents, contacts, plans, and contracts on a special intranet designed for just this purpose. And it kept Sean's most prized asset—his sanity—safe from harm.

Your Inheritance: What to Do When You're Given a Project

In a perfect world, a project manager would start a project and follow it through to its end, staying with it the entire time. But, in case you hadn't noticed, we live in a less-than-perfect world, and PMs rarely have this luxury. You're often given a project that was started before you even knew it existed, and you're told to finish it as efficiently—and cheaply—as possible.

Of course, the state of the project when you inherit it may not be what you'd like. In fact, it may not even be a "project." It may be a godawful mess—a poorly defined goal with a loose team assembled and no project management techniques in place. Your job, such as it is, may be to apply the project management discipline where none existed before it.

Or in contrast, you may walk into a project that *did* have a PM before you, only to find the PM and his work were shoddy. (Perhaps he was fired; perhaps that's why you're there.) The project charter, you find, is poorly written. There are few if any processes in place for change and scope management, and the scope document, the one indispensable form in any project, is missing altogether.

In any case, it's your job now, and your duty to bring the project you inherit up to par. So how do you do it? Don't panic; just follow the steps below.

> **Meet and greet** Remember, your most important asset on any project, no matter what it is, is your project team. Before you do anything, get to know them well. Start with a team meeting in which you introduce yourself and your background and encourage your team members to do the same. Then follow up one-on-one with each of them. Perhaps you'll take them to lunch. Perhaps you'll simply take a walk outside the office to get to know them better. (Remember, people tend to open up when they're outside the office, in a relaxed setting. This can be an invaluable tool for you if you're trying to get your hands around a project's scope and prior problems.)
>
> You need to do more, of course, than simply learn your team members' names and a snippet or two of their past. You need to learn what

each can do—his or her specialized skills—and how these impact your project as a whole. And you need to begin to judge their competence.

Assess Once you've met your project team, a process that can take no more than a few hours up to a few days depending on its size, you need to assess the state of the project. Chances are, the project's sponsor already gave you her assessment when she assigned you to head the project. So you won't be working in the dark. But now it's your time to make your own judgments.

Start by reading the project manual or library, if it exists. Are there weekly status reports? Read as many as you can. Is there a statement of scope? Learn it well (or draw one up if it doesn't exist). Have there been changes to the scope? Endeavor to understand what they are and why they exist. At this point you may need to go back to your project team, or simply to certain members thereof, and have an involved talk about the project's history. The question you're trying to answer, as deeply as possible, is why the project is where it is now. How did we get here?

Dream and scheme Now that you know where you are, and crucially, how you got there, it's time to take this baby forward. Start with a plan. You have a goal and a deadline to meet, so dream and scheme your way towards them. Write a project charter if there was none before. (If there was, revamp it until it meets your current needs.) Draw up a statement of scope and refine it until it perfectly reflects the size of your project. Start to institute project management practices like change and risk management. And run some of the exercises outlined in Chapter 4, such as the Pleasure and Displeasure List or the Myers-Briggs exam in Chapter 1.

The goal is simple: Even though you have a project in progress, treat it as if it were new (after all, it's new to you) and fill in the project management gaps (or gaping holes) that existed before you arrived on scene.

Just Do It With a plan in place and a healthy injection of project management discipline behind you, it's time for the rubber to meet the road. Put your plan into action and take your team forward. Start to accomplish your tasks one by one and work towards your goal. In time, you'll have a first-rate project under your belt, and you'll be hailed as a savior by your team and your bosses alike.

Getting It Right (The Second Time)

After four days in his 1992 Toyota Celica (in which there was no air or heat) and a stop in Cawker City, Kansas, to see the world's largest ball of twine, Mike D. and his new bride arrived in Trenton on Christmas Eve, 2000, where he was slated to start a new job after the first of the year.

His position? A techie on the IT staff at a paper recycling plant. In his first week his boss tasked him with upgrading the plant's phone system, which involved new software, equipment, and lines. Ever the optimist, Mike assumed the scope of the project had been finalized before he arrived, since he was given an equipment list and a stack of purchase orders that were already issued.

Silly Mike. When he began to review the new system's features with the employees, who wanted everything from caller ID to three-way calling and voice-over-IP, he began to get chills. This was news to him. So he turned to what he thought were the scope docs for the project and discovered, much to his dismay, that the requirements were vastly understated.

The budget he'd been given was a cool hundred grand, but despite the large amount, Mike, never slow on the uptake, knew it would never cover a system as complex as they needed. Over the next week he refined the scope document, budget, and schedule and reviewed the project with his boss. Yelling and screaming ensued, but after a time Mike convinced him to not fire the messenger.

A week later, after meetings with the CFO, the head of operations, and the facilities manager, not to mention a good deal of begging and pleading (at one point groveling was involved), Mike's revised project was approved.

Tuesday Morning News

Mondays—how shall we put this bluntly?—suck. You stumble into the office with the weekend's fog still over your head, sit at your desk, and with bleary eyes begin to sort your e-mail. But there's work to be done and work you'll do, starting, most likely, with meetings.

In fact, Mondays are choice days for meetings, starting with meetings on last week's progress (who did what, when, and with whom, and how it turned out) and moving into meetings on this week's plans, which is why Tuesday is such a good day for the news.

The Tuesday Morning News is simply a newsletter or bulletin you produce for a major project. It contains

- Recent updates

- Project news

- Resource requirements

- Schedules

- Personnel additions and deletions

- Company news

- Training information

- Task assignments for staff

- A financial report

- Any other information you deem important for your project team

You can produce it on paper (for you Luddites of the world), send it by e-mail, or post it to your project intranet.

Be a Type C Guy

Think of that cinema epic, *Butch Cassidy and the Sundance Kid*. Butch and Sundance keep asking the question, "Who are those guys? Really, just who are those guys?" referring to the elite posse dispatched to pursue them, as they peer out over the prairie and see the dust cloud of the posse hot on their heels. Well, "those guys," that posse, are known as Type C guys.

We've all heard of Type A personalities. Type A behavior is classically defined as an emotional response brought on by stress. It's believed to have its roots in Western cultural values that reward people who can produce with great amounts of speed, efficiency, and aggression. This type of behavior involves traits such as impatience, a sense of urgency, and the desire to achieve recognition and advancement. Type A people have an extreme awareness of time and therefore walk, eat, and perform most tasks quickly. They also tend to have traits such as facial tension, rapid speech, and tongue and teeth clicking.

Not so with Type Bs. These people—and they're less common than Type As—are good at relaxing. Not surprisingly, they can work hard but not get anxious or agitated. They're often lax about time (being late is no big deal to them), and they're slow to anger. The opposite of Type As, Type Bs are unhurried and satisfied; they're even serene.

So what kind of person deals with Type A and B people? Type Cs do. Type Cs thrive on taming chaos into calm structure. They live to create order and plan, which, when you think of it, sounds like the role of a PM, no?

Type C behavior was first defined by psychologist Perry W. Buffington, who now goes under the name of Dr. Buff. Dr. Buff outlines the following traits of Type C personalities.

Mess finding This one's simple. You realize you've got a mess on your hands (often, it's one you've inherited), and you try to see just how big the problem is.

Data finding You can't begin to clean up a mess until you know what the dilemma is. Hence the data-finding trait, in which you gather all the information surrounding the state of the mess.

Problem finding As you sift and sort the data, you'll begin to find the problems and rank them in order of priority.

Idea finding Type Cs rarely settle for a single idea. They brainstorm and come up with several—even dozens—for a given project.

Solution finding Ideas in hand, Type Cs review and rank them. Often two or three become viable solutions to the problem at hand.

Acceptance finding Once they've zeroed in on the best solution, Type Cs get other people involved. They market and sell their solution just like a product.

PMs tend to thrive in this type of arena. It's common for a PM to inherit a project that's already been "driven into the ditch off a dirt road." The car (that is, the project) just sits there in the mud, while all the passengers (the project team) stand around and half-heartedly think about how to get the car back on the road. Every now and then one of them will get in the car, crank it up and spin the tires in the mud, and then give up in a few minutes' time. Then and only then does the newly appointed PM arrive on his white horse and proceed to truly analyze the situation. With the help of his trusty steed, he quickly hauls the car up from the ditch and puts it firmly on the road. Using his superior communication and organizational skills, he brings the group together as a team and they zoom off to successfully complete their mission. So how 'bout a hand for those Type C guys?

PMs who are good at their craft truly thrive on resolving this chaos, solving the problem, accepting the high fives, and moving on to the next threat that will guarantee more thrills. Their approach is future-centered; they have a clear vision of the completed project and how to go about getting there.

The Skills Matrix

Like any good craftsman, PMs need to have the right tools for the job, but even more, they need to know the quality (and the availability) of what's in the tool chest.

Believe it or not, there was a time when the average PM ran several bulging teams at once, teams that could handle any project they came across. Overstaffed but not overextended, these teams were huge, and their members brought an abundance of skills to the projects they worked on. (You may have guessed that teams like these were par for the course in the over-indulgent 1980s, when "more" and "more extravagant" were de rigueur and American firms spent lavishly on personnel.)

Times change. Today "lean and mean" is the order of business, and teams are often assembled ad hoc, based on the needs of the project at hand. They rarely contain more people than needed, and the skills that team members bring to a project, while ample, are rarely enough to meet the full extent of the tasks at hand.

But one thing hasn't changed. The PM, despite the size of her team and the range of its skills, still has to deliver the goods. So what's a skilled PM to do? The answer is simple: Wring every last drop of talent from the team at hand. To that end, there are three steps to perform:

1. Assess your team's skills.

2. Train your team or bring in outside help.

3. Assign team members to tasks.

Assess your team's skills. First of all, what skills does the project need? During the project-planning phase, for instance, the PM has to identify the skills and technologies required to carry out the many project tasks that lay ahead. This should be done in as detailed a level as practical in what's called a *skills matrix*.

Start your team's skills matrix by making a chart with rows and columns. (In fact it's best to do this in a spreadsheet program, such as Excel. You can find a skills matrix template on the Herding Chickens website at www.herdingchickens.com.) You put skills in the rows and team members' names in the columns (see below).

The matrix should include three groups of skills: functional, technical, and human. Functional skills include legal, finance, distribution, programming, engineering, or a combination thereof. Technical skills include knowledge of certain software programs or the possession of a contractor's license. Lastly, your human skills include facilitator certification, or traits such as stress management or communications skills. They also include skills that are often overlooked, such as how to run a meeting or how to manage a project plan.

Then, in the table's cells, insert codes for each member of the team based on the skills he can perform. For example:

F—The team member is familiar with that program or skill set.

S—The team member is skilled at that function.

E—The team member is expert at that function.

Using the matrix, you can rapidly find any holes in the skills your project team needs (for instance, in the matrix below, no one knows Quick-Books, an essential team need), and you can hold your team members accountable for their skill level estimates.

Here's a sample skills matrix:

Skill	Sally	Jim	Peter	Dan	Brad	Joy	Sam
Contracts/Licensing	E		F				
QuickBooks Pro							
COBOL		E					
Microsoft Excel	F	E	S	S	S	F	F
Vendor Management	S			E		E	
Stress Management			F	S		S	E

Keep in mind that as the project evolves, the skills it demands of its team will change, and your matrix may change (or grow) as a result.

Train your team or bring in outside help. Once you've compiled the matrix, meet with your sponsor and review your team members' strengths, noting how each member can best help the project. Of course, you need to state your team's deficiencies too. Are there gaps in your technical skills, such as C++ or Basic? Do you need more legal help, say, with litigation?

With the skills matrix as your guide, you're now in a position to get your team some training, or, if there's no budget for training, find other people to fill in the gaps. Don't forget that contractors and consultants can be invaluable, above all when you're dealing with new technologies. And sometimes it's better to accept a part-time resource immediately—one you can hire as a vendor—rather than wait for a full-time person to arrive. (Of course, some tasks may be hard to carry out on a part-time basis.)

When should you take the time and money to train your staff, and when should you hire a SME to step in and fill a void in skills? Of course it depends. If you foresee a long-term need for a special skill (perhaps you're starting one of many software projects, and you'll need a coder who knows Java for the next two years), you'll need to train a team member to do it. On the other hand, if the skill in question is just needed once, it's cheaper—and simpler—to get some outside help in the short term.

Assign team members to tasks. The last phase, assignment, is easy. Simply assign a team member to a task set based on his skill set.

Of course, not everyone in your enterprise will fully respect your schedule, and assign you the key people just when you need them. In fact, you may have to fight the Powers That Be to get the right people assigned for your team. What's more, your team members may be pulled back to their home base—and away from your team—before their involvement in your project is finished. If that happens, you'll need to play the diplomat (and perhaps the pushy hard-ass) to negotiate for more of their time and talents.

Shut It Down/Turn It Around

Shutdown/turnaround projects have been around for decades. They're nearly as old as Dick Clark. They began as maintenance projects in huge industrial plants, but the concept expanded to projects such as computer or network changeovers, the installation of new communications systems, and other projects that run on a short fuse. What defines them? Simple: The execution of these projects is very quick, with durations measured in minutes and hours instead of days and weeks. What's more, the downtime inherent in shutdown/turnaround projects can often be measured in hundreds (if not thousands) of dollars per minute in lost revenues. Careers, including yours, can easily be made or lost in this cauldron of high-pressure.

So, do we have your attention? Good, because it's vital to manage shutdown/turnaround projects as tightly as possible. And you've got two choices to manage them:

- First, you can seek out PMs who've been there and done that based on their experience, personality, and sheer will, and then rely on them to run the shutdown/turnaround project with exacting precision, or

- Second, you can develop new systems and procedures that don't depend on the availability of a particular manager.

Of the two, the second option is better. If you develop new systems to run your shutdown/turnaround project, it removes the burden of improvising on the fly and ensures that operations will continue even in the absence of key managers or team members (say, when one of them is assigned away from your team).

Note the following comparison of "regular" projects and shutdown/turnarounds:

On a "Regular" Project	On a Shutdown/Turnaround Project
The scope is relatively static. Few changes may occur during the implementation.	Although scope may be well-defined initially, during implementation, scope can change hourly or daily due to unexpected work results during execution.

On a "Regular" Project	On a Shutdown/Turnaround Project
Planning can be done well in advance.	Planning and scheduling can only be finalized immediately before shutdown.
Projects are organized around areas and systems.	Turnarounds are time-based.
By and large, staffing needs are stable.	Staffing may change quickly due to scope changes.
Time is measured in days, weeks, and months.	Time is measured in hours or minutes.
Staffing may change quickly due to scope changes.	Schedules must be updated almost hourly.

As you can see from this table, time is of the essence in shutdown/turnaround projects, and the PM must use critical-path techniques as well as visuals and graphics to schedule every step of the process.

As for graphics, the PM may want to use a *storyboard*, as seen below, that outlines tasks in the shutdown/turnaround and depicts exactly what needs to happen on the most detailed of levels. These are techniques that might not be used (or used as extensively) in a "regular" project, where schedules are not as tight.

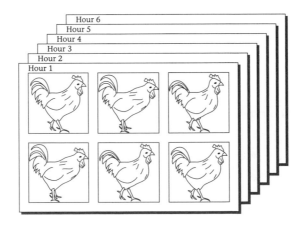

We'd love to ramble on and on about critical path, which is an essential skill for shutdown/turnarounds and nearly all other projects, but that's a subject for a book of its own. For now, we'll merely say that as the critical-path method is highly analytical, all activities are sequenced and prioritized in a logical and efficient manner. This approach also lets you develop a number of "what if" scenarios, because you don't have time to develop these once the shutdown is underway. The net result is a realistic, workable, if highly detailed schedule that can be met.

The substantial savings involved in properly organizing, planning, scheduling, and controlling a shutdown/turnaround project easily justify the cost and effort required. Keep in mind that for these types of projects, time is of the essence. The alternative—to let a turnaround run its course without thorough preplanning, estimating, and organizing—is a costly one, as lost minutes can equal thousands, if not tens of thousands, of dollars. And if you're the PM in charge of the job, your boss will take it right out of your own pocket—or your scalp.

Chapter 4

Surviving the Corporate Jungle

Yes, it's a jungle out there. You can know project management back and forth, up and down, and sideways, but still be felled by office politics or a quirky sponsor. You can write the finest budgets, draft the best schedules, and manage the mechanics of time and money like no one else in the world, and still be harmed by an unruly team or an office Rasputin. Buck up, friend: It's just the way of the world.

But it's not a law you have to abide by. In fact, if you're smart about human dynamics and the workings of egos, you can slash your way through the jungle without breaking a sweat. How? We'll show you.

Finessing the Project Sponsor

Heads up, PMs! The next time you start a new project, draft a little memo to your sponsor that reads something like this:

Dear Project Sponsor:

> *Congratulations on being our sponsor. I know this project won't be a success without your skills and involvement. Your mission is to provide support to me and my team, to champion our efforts and provide the high-level exposure to your executive network that our project deserves.*

> *As you work the corporate bureaucracy to give us strategic plans and guidance, you'll constantly keep the organization's focus on the relevance and value of our project, both today and in the future. Your skills in obtaining sufficient funds (or more than sufficient funds) will let our team deliver a world-class project. Your steadfast defense of our project plan in front of the executive steering committee will let us move unhindered towards a common goal.*

> *Please let me know your suggestions and thoughts. As always, I look forward to working together.*

Yours,
Aiden Bryce, PM

Now that you've gotten your sponsor on board, keep working with him—and on him. Why? Because once you've gotten a good sponsor (remember: a good one), you don't want to lose him. You never know when something may take him out of the game.

Believe it or not, it happens more than you think, most often on projects with long durations, say, two years or more. It's not uncommon for a project to finish with a different sponsor than it started with due to promotion, reassignment, sickness, layoffs, or more. It's sad, but your sponsor may just lose interest in your project and hang you out to dry.

There are plenty of ways you can prepare for the unfortunate (but not unheard-of) departure of your sponsor. Like any good PM, you should have a backup plan in place. First, use your own political network to ensure that your project has widespread support within your firm. Have an eye-to-eye meeting, early on, with your sponsor and let him know of your commitment to your project, and, in no uncertain terms, the commitment that you expect from him in return. Follow the meeting with a memo like the one above that reviews the subjects you discussed, in the event that he's not holding up his end of the project. It's called a *memo to file*. So when your sponsor underperforms, as he may very well do, pull out your memo and jog his memory.

Put your backup plan into action, too. Don't back down: If you must, jump in as interim sponsor while you shop the company for a new one. Once a new sponsor comes on board, treat his arrival like the advent of a new project. Have a new kickoff meeting to acquaint the newbie and reinvigorate your team.

Of course, there are ways your sponsor can harm your project besides leaving it. Here are just a few of them:

- Use your project budget to fund sundry expenses from other projects that are over budget.

- If the project is running over budget and behind schedule, disown any knowledge of it and make you the scapegoat.

- Arrive in the middle of status meetings and stay five minutes or less before rushing out for something more important.

- Refuse to meet with the team during the early planning phase, then telepathically send his ideas to them and berate them for not asking for input.

- Always corner a minor team member and ask him, "Just between you and me, how's this sham of a project going?"

Do you have problems like these? If so, the best course of action may lie in ditching your sponsor. It's not as hard as it seems. A sponsor who disowns your project, skips your meetings or simply comes late to them, or badgers minor team members for gossip wants out of your project to start with. Actions speak louder than words, and those actions are fairly screaming. So on the QT, approach a new sponsor and secure his support. Find someone you know and trust, or merely someone whose interests dovetail with yours (though it's clear the former is better). Once you've got his support, go to your current sponsor and say that so-and-so has an interest in "giving us help, and would you mind?" (Whatever you do, don't use the phrase "taking over" or "stepping in;" they both have overtones you want to avoid.) Your current sponsor (who's eager to bail as it is) will rarely mind. In fact, nine times out of 10, he'll be all too happy to cede his control, leaving you free and clear to invite your new sponsor into the mix.

The Pleasure and Displeasure List

Sometimes, all that matters is whom you tick off and whom you please.

Let's rephrase that for accuracy. *Most of the time*, all that matters is whom you tick off and whom you please. Your project rides on it. Why? Because we know that projects are run by people. Hence projects are politics. It's just the nature of the beast. If you don't like it, you're not a project manager. PMs spend most of their time communicating. Get used to it or get out of the game.

Yet for so clear and simple a truth, so many PMs ignore it like the plague. We plan our schedules and *work breakdown structures (WBS)* with a precision that rivals lab work, but we ignore the basic rules of power consistently. Why? Largely because we're stupid.

Let's stop being stupid. At the start of your next project—say, at your project kickoff meeting—run this exercise with your team. You're about to draw a chart. On the left-hand side of a sheet of paper, list all the people who can affect your project's outcome. Now, across the top of the page, write the words *Pleasure* and *Displeasure* to form two columns, and fill in the chart:

Person/Group	Pleasure	Displeasure
Marketing Department	Recognition of website and print collaterals	Lack of input and feedback from sales team
CEO	Project on time and on budget	Project updates requesting more project funds; delays
IT Director	Flexibility regarding software vendors	Dictating specific vendors and costs
Editor	Exquisite writing	Lack of communication

We show a blank of this form in the Appendix. You can find a template for your use on the Web at www.herdingchickens.com.

When you fill in your *Pleasure and Displeasure List*, figure out what's going to put a smile on your CEO's face (what's *legitimately* going to put a smile on his face, that is: You don't want to brownnose) and write it in the Pleasure box. Of equal importance, figure out what's going to tick the man off, and write it in the Displeasure box. These become your team's rules for the duration of the project, and if you're smart, even beyond.

(A note: If you're not sure what's going to make someone happy, or what's going to upset him, just ask. Don't rely on assumptions. As the saying goes, when you assume something, you make an *ass* out of *u* and *me*.)

Remember to approach the list with the mindset of a coach. Your job is to use it to hone your team's political skills. You want to coach them to be more sensitive to nuance and subtlety in office politics, while using the list to ensure a better outcome, or set of outcomes, for your project.

The "Don't Know, Can't Do, Won't Do" Rule

Some of us work like dogs, others goof off, and some are just along for the ride. How many times have you heard one of these?

"Sorry, I don't know how to do that."

"I can't do that. It's out of my job description."

"I asked Mike to do it three different times, but he won't. He says it's not his job."

Statements like these are part of the "Don't Know, Can't Do, Won't Do" Rule, the notion that some people in your office will always be less than happy to help get your projects done. They're not bad people. In fact, if you knew them well, you might learn they have friends and families and children and good, caring lives. But once they step foot in the office, they become 9-to-5 drones who do only what they have to and nothing more, just what they need to get by. For them, there's no such thing as "the extra mile." There's no such thing as "bending over backwards." In fact, there's no bending at all: They're rigid and tight with their work, and they're not about to help you with yours.

We've all known people like these. There's just something about the nature of American corporate cultures that tends to breed them—*en masse*. And we've all dealt with their impact on projects: missed deadlines, budgets that get fat and bloated, and work that barely meets the standards for competence. The question is, how do you deal with them? How do you turn a sloth into a cheetah, ready to run the plains and track down the prey of project goals and deadlines?

You don't. You can't. The main trait of "Don't Know, Can't Do, Won't Do" workers is an inbred incorrigibility: They're averse to change and they're about as flexible as a piece of tempered steel. The trick to getting the most from them—and letting them do as little damage as possible—is in making careful task assignments.

As the PM, it's your job to outline the scope of the work on your project. That much we all know. But it's also your job to say who does what and when. It's your job to *assign* tasks as much as it's your job to come up with them in the first place. And, when dealing with "Don't Know, Can't Do,

Won't Do" workers, you need to make special efforts not to assign them to crucial tasks. Give those to your stars, your lieutenants, and your ambitious and hungry souls. Let the others do the humdrum jobs that no one else wants; they'll be glad to busy themselves with busy work—it's less taxing—and they'll be pleased to lose themselves in useless and dull minutiae.

Of course, there are times when some of your senior SMEs and other team members are "Don't Know, Can't Do, Won't Do" workers. In fact, there are times when your sponsors hew to this rule with a religious zeal. And those are times when you're in trouble. You need their work and input, which can be crucial, and they're out to lunch five days a week, eight hours a day.

If you find yourself stuck with a dud in a key position on your project team, it's time to play the politician. First, do what you can to make the dud perform: Check in frequently, send him reminders, give him offers of help, and have others do the same. (It's an irony of the "Don't Know, Can't Do, Won't Do" Rule: Often the people who contribute least to your projects are those who take up the most of your time and help.) Second, assign him only those tasks you must; limit his scope of work in radical ways, as much as you can without causing offense. And third, shop around for a replacement. If you have four lawyers in your firm and the one who's assigned to your project is as lazy as a tick, find a way to get a different lawyer on your team. There may, of course, be no way to do that, but more often than not, you can find a reason to justify a switch. Maybe one of the other lawyers has special knowledge you'll need for your project. Maybe the lawyer assigned to your team is best suited to another project in progress. Whatever the reason, find one and use it as leverage to better your team.

In the end, you—and your projects—will be the better for it. Remember that it's just as vital to manage your people and their drive, ambition, and labor as it is to manage your time and budget. In fact, it may be more important: If you can manage your people well, attracting the best and brightest to your team, you'll find it's simpler to manage your time and budget as a result. As we've said before, projects are people—and the better your people, the better your projects.

Planning for Crisis

The business of *crisis management* goes under several names: *disaster recovery (DR)*, *contingency planning (CP)*, and *business continuity planning (BCP)*, to name a few. But for each, the bottom line is the same: Write and put contingency plans in place, just in case the worst comes to pass.

Crisis management is not to be confused with *risk management* or *risk planning*, which is a standard part of any project. Crisis management, disaster recovery, contingency planning, and business continuity planning are whole projects in themselves. They apply to the enterprise as a whole, and instead of making plans for standard and sometimes minor risks, you're making plans for massive problems such as fires, floods, or the death of a key executive.

Major data-intensive companies have been doing this for decades, realizing the impact on their operations if a major data center went down, say, in California, with its fancy for earthquakes. These companies will mirror a data center on the East Coast. The cost to do this, of course, is huge. But the cost of not doing it, should a disaster occur, is worse. In fact, it's so awful that a company might be forced out of business.

So how does project management apply to the collective field of DR, CP, and BCP? First, the job of writing a disaster plan is often assigned to a project manager, who assembles a team from all corners of the enterprise and coordinates its work. And second, in writing contingency plans, you're simply planning out different scenarios—most of them hellish—that may occur in the future, and planning, as we know, is at the heart of project management.

The whole concept of contingency planning, which is now a large and growing field of specialization, began with the idea of simple *disaster recovery*—in other words, how to quickly assess the damage to a company and resume some form of limited operations after a hurricane, earthquake, blackout, or other major disaster. In fact, there's even a magazine, *The Disaster Recovery Journal*, which provides a forum for articles and discussions of lessons learned, planning, and allocating resources for this effort.

The *business continuity plan (BCP)* is what you'll turn to if there is, indeed, a major disaster at your firm. A BCP is a comprehensive statement of actions you'll take before, during and after a disaster, and should focus on the following:

- Minimizing the disruption of day-to-day operations

- Keeping the company stable

- Providing for an orderly recovery after the disaster

- Providing a sense of security

- Guaranteeing the reliability of standby systems

With luck you'll never have to use your BCP, but if you do, it can be your saving grace, the difference between the complete loss of your company and its stalwart survival. Hence it's crucial that your plan be simple, clear, workable, and sufficiently detailed to guide you through the crisis.

The BCP should

- Include a commitment from executive management.

- Establish a planning team.

- Perform a business impact analysis (see below).

- Establish priorities of operations (in other words, which departments and functions must come back online first).

- Determine recovery strategies.

- Be tested with objective measures of success. (These include time to network restoration and other metrics.)

This last point is crucial. After you've written your BCP, you should test the plan with dry runs and drills and have it approved by the CEO, president, or director of operations.

One of the key steps in writing a smart BCP is noting the potential impact of *each type of problem* you might encounter, not merely fires, floods, and storms. (After all, you can't plan for disaster if you don't plan for every disaster that could impact your business.) This means disasters you may not have thought of, but should: terror, earthquakes, a long power outage (such as the New England blackout of 2003), the death of a key executive, and more. It's surprising how many companies bypass this initial step in the planning process, called *business impact analysis*.

Business impact analysis is simply a means of systematically assessing the potential impact of potential disasters. The business impact analysis is intended to help you develop and understand the degree of possible loss that could occur when disaster strikes your business. This will cover not just direct financial loss, but other issues such as the loss of customer support, the impact on product shipping, and so on.

When you write your BCP, be sure to include more than offsite storage or backup data processing. You should address *all* the critical operations and functions of the business. In addition, the plan should include documented and tested procedures, which, if followed, will ensure the ongoing availability of critical resources and continuity of operations.

You never know when disaster will strike. A disaster plan, however, is a bit like liability insurance: It offers a certain level of comfort in knowing that a fire or flood won't cause financial ruin for your company. But insurance alone is not enough, because it may not compensate for the incalculable loss of business during the interruption—or worse, the business that never returns from the brink of destruction.

Managing Change

Whoever said, "The only thing constant is change," got it utterly right. In the mid-90s this simple truth was raised to a new level by the management consultant gurus of the day, who gave birth to the *change management* movement.

Now, by change management, we're not referring to managing change on a single project, or even on a group of projects. The term, as it's used here, applies to managing change across the enterprise—that is, changing the very way your company works. You might, for instance, change the way you do customer service (perhaps you're adding a new call center), or change your procedures for employee background checks. This is change management at the enterprise level.

This type of change may vary in scope and scale, and it may focus on small or large groups, one or more divisions or departments, the entire company, or strictly on one or more aspects of the company's outside environment, such as social and political upheaval, the actions of competitors, changing economic tides, and more.

As a result of all this change, and despite the progress of the change management movement, most firms are still highly frustrated over the time it takes to implement change itself. Why? Because, by and large, there's lots of talk but little action when it comes to handling change at the most basic, core levels of a firm, and when the action does come, it's often a knee-jerk response without a well-conceived plan for implementation.

Enter project management. When it comes to changing the way a business runs, and changing the very functions of business departments, project management is the silver bullet.

We'll explain. Most firms that live through dramatic change have always faced unforeseen (and sometimes unwanted) problems in managing that change. Say your firm wants to overhaul its customer service process. As part and parcel of that change, you're installing a new call center and adding live chat to your website. Sounds great, and it is—until the phones you bought for the call center turn out to be defective, and the website gets swamped with so many hits from so many users that you can't keep up with demand, thus ticking your customers off and—a sad irony—ending up with even worse customer service than you started with.

But problems like this—and indeed, the whole change management process itself—are perfectly suited for project management techniques. Why? Because change management can be split into the following steps:

- The current state

- The transition phase

- The future state

And these are common to all projects. In all projects we start with the *current state*, which is simply how things exist at the moment, before there's any move to change them. At times the current state is a void, for instance, a raw tract of land where a building will stand in two years' time. Or, for a systems platform changeover, the current state is a platform (such as Windows or Linux) that a project team will replace with a new system.

The *transition phase* is where all the work happens, where things move from A, the current state, to B, the future state. It's also the phase where PM techniques can make the most difference. After all, the transition phase is nothing but a project in progress. (And hence the transition phase of a change management process is nearly always run by a seasoned project manager.) For the uninformed, activity during this phase may seem chaotic, with no underlying plan. And some people fear the transition phase so much they insist on staying in their current, familiar state (for example, refusing to work in Linux and insisting on staying in Windows), despite the fact they know it's not optimal. But in truth, the project management team has a concrete plan for getting from point A to point B, and while the transition may seem troubling to some, it's really an orderly process of change.

The *future state* is simply the project's end point, when you assess your work, conduct the post mortem (see Chapter 3, "Tips Not Typically Taught"), disband the team, and move on to the next project.

Of course, projects themselves undergo change. Plans change; needs change; it's simply a certainty. In fact for some projects your scope can change day by day. Those of you who think it won't—or think your project plan is sacrosanct merely because you wrote it—are in for a bleak surprise (and maybe more than one). So the effective PM is not responsible for planning the perfect project, but instead, for planning to minimize the effect of those unforeseen bumps as they occur. As the project progresses, most of the pitfalls that do occur are not the making of the PM, but he must anticipate and deal with them effectively or else the project will suffer.

So, the next time that you hear of some major change initiative about to take place in your company, just point them to the methodologies that PMs use to effectively run their projects. It's not rocket science, merely a structured approach to get from the current state to the future state. And it works.

Matrix Management

Matrix...it's a movie, right?

Yup. But it's also the name of an approach to management that works in companies with several large projects underway at once.

Typically, large companies have autonomous divisions that rarely need to deal with one another. (This holds true for big firms, the Fortune 1000, and other national—and international—outfits. It's not so common in the less daunting world of local shops and not-for-profits.) Management in a big company is often simplified, in that you have only one boss, who has only one boss, who has only one boss, and so on, all the way up to the top. People rarely report to more than one person. And while this has its benefits, it makes it hard to run projects that cross the lines between divisions. In a traditional management structure, there's no one person or group to champion the project across the enterprise, that is, across divisional lines. It's simply the nature of the beast, the hallmark of the corporate culture: People work in isolated little islands (teams) that are part of an archipelago (the division), but they rarely travel from one chain of islands to the next.

Not so in a matrixed company, where employees are temporarily assigned to interdepartmental projects, but remain on the payroll of their functional department. It's typically in their departments that employees receive their employment reviews, promotions, and overall supervision. See the diagram below:

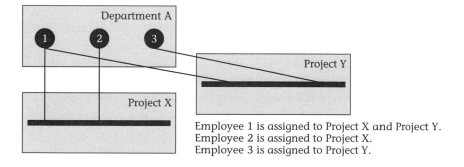

Employee 1 is assigned to Project X and Project Y.
Employee 2 is assigned to Project X.
Employee 3 is assigned to Project Y.

This diagram reflects the reporting structure of a matrixed company running multiple projects. A person working in Department A but assigned part-time to Projects X and Y will find that he reports to three different managers, all of whom have some control over him. That may sound daunting at first, but it's not: It simply means that in the matrixed firm, you report to different people for different jobs.

Depending upon the size and complexity of the project, the employee may be moved to a certain area with other team members, or he may stay in his home department. Projects tend to benefit from this type of management, but, as with most things, there's a downside: The PM has little authority to hire, fire, or promote the members of a matrixed team. For that reason alone she must use the full range of her communication and management skills to get the assigned team members to cooperate and work as one.

How? As follows:

- Never forget the importance of the project kickoff meeting. It's the first time you'll bring your team together, and since your matrixed team includes people from all kinds of departments—people who've rarely met one another before—the kickoff meeting is as important as air.

- For that matter, weekly meetings (for status reports, planning, or merely team-building) are useful as well. They keep people in touch with each other. They keep relationships fresh. And they encourage coordination. You might want to avoid weekly meetings with a non-matrixed team, since they're time-consuming and perhaps too frequent. But with the matrixed, multi-department team, they're a *sine qua non*.

- If you need to, spend time on team-building tasks and jobs that get your team to think as a group about project goals. These include the Pleasure and Displeasure List described earlier in this chapter (a template for which is available in the Appendix and at www.herdingchickens.com).

- Get to know the heads of the departments that your team comes from. Given, this can take some time when you've got a large team whose members hail from several departments. But it's vital that your team members know you speak with the authority of their primary boss. After all, you may not be able to hire, fire, promote, or demote your team members, but you can manage them better when they know you speak to their superiors.

High Voltage

An electric company had been around for the better part of a century and was on the verge of massive expansion, since its state saw the influx of thousands of new people each day. As a company, it was an old place that worked by old rules. The lines of authority were cast in stone, the org chart was inviolate, and everyone in the firm had one and only one boss. Even the dress code was old-fashioned, a relic from the 1950s.

Whenever it was time to build a new transmission line, many departments—Marketing, Land Acquisition, Substation Engineering, Construction, Lines and Rights-of-Way, and Commercial Sales, to name a few—had to pitch in. Each had a specific task to do, but rather than form matrixed teams to coordinate the process, each department would do its job and "throw it over the wall" to the next department. The result? There was no rhyme or reason to which task, much less which project, got done first. Departments and teams simply focused on their own workload with no regard for the way their output affected the schedules of other groups. Deadlines were missed. Clients were angry. And even the workers themselves were flummoxed. Once, construction of a transmission line was brought to an abrupt stop three miles into the woods from its destination, because the Land Acquisition group did not plan to acquire the land rights to complete the line for another six months.

Enter Tyler M., an MBA fresh out of Tuck with a reputation for revolution. He was hired to replace an aging VP of operations whose management style was as fresh as day-old bread.

For new transmission lines (there were roughly 200 in the works), Tyler adopted a process in which each department assigned a member to a project team, with each of the members reporting directly to a seasoned PM. Each PM ran 10 projects, most of which varied only in the details such as location, cost of installation, and so on. The team members were charged with coordinating the work of their home departments, and, as a result, things began to improve. Projects were not merely done (a new feeling for quite a few team members), but done *well*. Clients were happy. And Tyler was given a five-figure bonus. ✒

The ABCs of Office Politics

Work is war. Sad, we know, but true: We've never found an office that's free of Svengalis and Rasputins. In fact we'll bet that you know a few of your own; they may be in the cubicle next to yours. Maybe you work for one. (If so, you have our sympathies.)

You'll need to know how to deal with them, as well as with the regular boys and girls whose agendas, egos, and wills can trample your day—and your project. Short of reading *The Prince*, you can brush up on your office politics with the tips below.

> **Don't gossip.** God knows most people do, but there's no good reason you should. Surveys have shown that office gossip is truly an office sport, with more than 80 percent of employees engaging in a little tongue-wagging now and then. But if you're not careful—and on occasion, even if you are—gossip can turn around and bite you from behind. What you say about others almost always gets back to them.
>
> If you must gossip—if it's simply ingrained in your DNA—then never, ever gossip about a sponsor or the executive in charge of your project. We guarantee he'll find out. He always does. And while he may not accost you directly (some people prefer to bear a grudge, and let it fester in secret), you can bet that you won't get the promotion you thought you would (and you won't get an honest reason for being declined). Either that, or you'll be poorly evaluated, or you'll be assigned to the worst projects there are.
>
> Now, all that said, there's no reason you can't *listen* to gossip as long as you don't engage in it yourself. (Some of you will argue that passive listening is enough to be called "engaging" in gossip, but we'll let you split that hair.) The office grapevine can be the best source of information on power relationships, project status, and the real issues that drive your projects along. So learn to listen without talking. And become a repository of information. But if you know what's good for you, you'll keep your mouth shut.

When you say "No," mean it. Look, there's not enough time in the day, no matter how good you are at writing lists and getting things done. So don't let people run you over with bad requests that leech your time, talent, and energy. If someone asks you for something you can't do, politely refuse.

Note the *politely*. Be firm, but don't be a bastard: Don't be abrupt or rude. Keep your voice calm and gentle. And whatever you do, don't dither. Believe it or not, people are often happy to accept a simple, honest "No" than to be told to wait for an answer (*Let me think about it* or *I'll let you know tomorrow*), only to get a rejection the next day.

If you have trouble saying no, get up your gumption. You won't make it far if you can't strengthen your spine. And remember: You're not rejecting the person who's doing the asking; you're just rejecting his request. There's nothing personal about that. (See our next rule: Be assertive, not aggressive.)

Be assertive, not aggressive. Yes, it's a careful balance, but one you can strike with some practice. Don't let people trample you in meetings or any other venue, for that matter, but in like kind, don't run over others in your attempt to have your way. Otherwise put: Stand up for yourself, but don't be overly forceful. Be persuasive. No one likes an ass.

In truth, most of us aren't assertive enough, in particular when it comes to rebuffing the boss. Here's a quick test to see if you are: Your boss, who's an all-around schmuck, tells you to work late for the fourth time this week, but you've told your son that you'll be at his soccer game at six o'clock sharp. What do you do? Do you

A. Tell your boss you need to leave to see your son, and much as you'd like to stay you simply can't?

B. Tell him you have to leave, but to make it up to him, you'll come to work early tomorrow?

C. Call your son and tell him not to expect you, as you'll be working late?

C is a copout. *B* is a politic, if self-effacing, answer. *A* is the right choice, so long as you do it firmly and politely. True, there are jobs that require you to give up your life and your family to boot (working at the White House comes to mind). But it's likely you don't have one of those jobs. Try to remember that.

Likewise, be assertive when asking for something. Don't apologize. Avoid lines like "I'm sorry to ask you this," or "I'd never ask, but...." Just state your case as plainly and politely as possible, and don't be cowed.

Offer solutions, not problems. The art of business is rife with problems; it's just the nature of business. Budgets are broken, schedules dumped, and people quit. (Or worse, they hang around when they should quit.) The truth is, if you're any good at business, you're good at solving problems. Look at it this way: Projects are nothing but large problems to be solved.

Of course, most people wallow in problems: They complain about them, rail against them, and shunt them off to others. So don't. Instead, be exceptional. Be one of the few people in your firm who never talks of a problem without offering a solution, *especially when you're talking to your project sponsor.* Don't bring him a problem without bringing him a few options to solve it. Over time, he'll come to look at you with respect. He'll think you're reliable. He'll know he can trust you.

Watch out for emotional e-mail. Trust us. It's all too easy to send off an angry e-mail in response to something you've just received. That's the problem with e-mail: It's too easy to send. It does little to promote self-control and calm language.

Of course, when you do flame someone by e-mail, you not only piss him off, but you preserve your bad behavior (and bad judgment, and lack of self-control) in the wires of your firm for eternity. And it can be read by network admins and the brass. (Remember: Any e-mail you write on the company network is company property, and open to review by any number of people you work for, or with.) What's more, if your project ever comes under audit, your e-mails and anything else you've written could be carefully scrutinized.

So what should you do, grasshopper? This: Instead of dashing off a red-hot reply and sending it now, write your reply and save it in the Drafts section of your e-mail software. Then come back to it an hour later (two is better), after you've cooled your heels. You'll tone it down. Then and only then should you send it.

And for God's sake, watch out who you send your e-mail to. All too often we've seen a team member send an off-color e-mail to the entire project team (or even the whole firm!) when he only meant to send it to one person. Ouch!

Don't whine. Every office has a whiner (some have more than one). These are people who complain *ad nauseam* and do nothing to better their problems. They take up time and leech energy. They bring people down. They're corrosive.

Don't be one of them. It may be hard, but "shut up and suffer" is a good piece of advice to keep in mind. Simply be stoic. People will notice, and your reputation for calm strength will precede you.

What's more, it's the job of PMs to deal with dozens of problems a day. You have schedules to fix, budgets to mend, and every kind of minor disaster to care to. Your team looks to you for guidance in the face of adversity. So don't open your mouth and scream at the wind. Learn to fly with the currents.

Bury the hatchet. Feuds are useless. They drain you of time and talent and worse, they're fodder for office gossip. Be neither a Hatfield nor a McCoy.

Instead, do whatever you can to bury the hatchet. If all else fails, try a sit-down meeting out of the office—over lunch or coffee is good. Buy your "enemy" a drink and offer to forget the past, while asking that he do the same. And whatever you do, don't start to rehash old history. Instead, find a point of common interest and suggest a small joint project around it. Small, because you want something that won't sap much of your time and won't do much damage if it fails. And joint, so you can do more than simply say you've buried the hatchet; you can actively work together towards a goal.

As the team leader, the PM also has to make her team play nice. If you've got team members who'd like to rip each other's eyes out, sit them down and force them to work out their problems. You've got too much stuff to worry about without having fights and squabbles mangle your day, and if you expect your project to work, to be completed on time and on budget, you need your team to play nice.

Beware extended leaves. If you have a job of any importance—and PMs are always important—don't be gone from the office for too long, on sick leave or otherwise. You can be made redundant in your absence, and office politicos can move in on your turf.

If you must be absent, have your stand-in send you copies of status reports, action item reports, and any changes to the project charter or statement of scope. That way you can stay on top of things, and put in your two cents by phone or e-mail when needed.

Delegate carefully. Face it: It's tempting to hand off the ball when you can. It saves you time, and sometimes it saves you headaches as well. But if you've got employees below you—such as your team members, who look to you for guidance and task assignments—you've got to be careful about what you delegate. You may want to give them menial or mindless tasks that were given to you, and as the team leader, you have that right. But no one wants to be told to be slavish; people want meaningful work. Don't make them feel like they're sweeping the floors.

Of course, at the same time, you need to be careful to keep certain tasks for yourself, key tasks that define your job. If you pass off important work to a subordinate and he does it well (and less expensively: his salary is smaller than yours) then your project sponsor may well begin to wonder about your value.

One of the problems with delegating work—and a cause of strife and conflict—is that it's often done incorrectly. When you do delegate, give careful directions, in writing if needed. Or better yet, ask your employee to write down the directions you've given to him, then e-mail them to you for review. (Just be careful not to patronize.)

Last, don't be a perfectionist, especially with others' work. There's no value to perfectionism in the work place. The best is often the enemy of the good, and people hate to be corrected. It builds resentment and sometimes rancor.

Give credit where credit is due. Don't be a tightwad with your praise. If someone does something right, let him know, and let him know in public, in front of others. Team meetings are the perfect time for PMs to spread the good word.

Just one caveat: Don't be effusive and don't flatter. People sense this inherently and it will only do you harm. There's no plus to insincerity.

Admit your mistakes. Few people ever do. Those who do are a cut above the rest, so why not be one? Yes, it's hard to swallow your pride and admit you're wrong, but if you do you'll gain the begrudging respect of your project team. Or at the very least you'll avoid their resentment.

Give critiques in private. If and when you have to rip someone a new one, do it behind closed doors. It's hard enough to be rebuked; it stings all the more when it's done in public. Never use a team meeting to point out a team member's failures. And when you do have to critique someone's work, use a calm voice and a gentle manner. Never, ever speak in anger. Wait till you're calm before you let forth with harsh words.

Learn to put it in writing. There are times when you need to cover your ass. Maybe you're having a conflict with a colleague and you need a record of what you've said and what he's said. Maybe you've told a sponsor that a project will be late, and you need to document it. Whatever the case, learn when to communicate by voice and when to do it in writing.

Learn *not* to put it in writing.   That said, there are times when you want to keep things off the written page, precisely because you *don't* want them saved for posterity. For instance, if you have to approach a colleague about handling your difficult boss (say, to strategize or give each other support), then do it in a conversation, and preferably one that's out of the office. Don't put it in e-mail and for Pete's sake, don't use a memo. There's a good chance that someone's watching (and reading), maybe even your boss herself.

The Godzilla Principle

Let's talk monsters. Big, bad ugly ones. In the movie *Jurassic Park* (the first one, before it spawned a God-awful franchise), a group of scholars are led through a lab on a clandestine island off Costa Rica where dinosaurs are born and bred. (Or is that hatched and bred? No matter.) The point is, they get to the raptor cage, where baby raptors are first poking their snouts through their eggs, and promptly fall in love with the little things. They're cute and almost cuddly. They make little baby reptile sounds.

Later in the film, the raptors grow up and eat nearly everyone in a bath of blood and guts.

Now let's switch to *Godzilla* (which, if you can believe it, was a worse film than *Jurassic Park*). Godzilla began her life (yes, the monster's a female; don't ask us why) as an adorable little lizard. Left unchecked, she grew in size and ate Tokyo without so much as a belch.

The same goes for minor problems, the kind you face every day at work: Left unchecked and uncared for, they wax, not wane, until they're too big to handle, until they're too big to solve. Thus it's best to check them when they're small. If not, you'll have a monster of a problem to deal with, and who wants that lizard on his back?

••

Splitsville

Divorce can be deadly. Husbands and wives once deeply in love can fight like Christians and tigers in a Roman arena. Children get hurt and lawyers get fat. But when a divorce is looming between members of your project team, you can add the project itself to the list of victims.

In 2003 Mel and Rita K. were key members of The H Group's legal team, part of a gaggle of lawyers assigned to defend the massive firm (H Group had 9,000 workers in the U.S. alone, and more than double that overseas) from a patent infringement lawsuit. Mel was a patent lawyer with a penchant for golf and a master's degree in physics; Rita, an awesome courtroom presence who often had her way with juries.

They'd been married for two years, in which time they'd been to Australia, New Zealand, Taiwan, Malaysia, and up and down the Indian coast, twice.

But in June their boss, Tom R., noticed something wrong: Mel began to skip meetings that Rita attended. And Rita, whose office was next to Mel's (and who'd always seemed to like the arrangement), began to work in the library. They never took lunch together. And once, when Tom asked Mel about Rita, he merely shrugged and changed the subject.

His suspicion piqued, Tom waited patiently for a joint brief that Mel and Rita were slated to file. This was no mean brief: At base, it argued a point of law—the interpretation of the Lanham Act—that could make or break the case. And tens of millions of dollars rode on the verdict.

As time passed Tom grew more worried. With only a week till deadline, he asked for the brief but got no response from Rita. He turned to Mel, leaving voicemail on voicemail, but they went unanswered. He began to haunt the halls in search of them. He even sent an intern to their house, but she rang the bell and no one answered.

Needless to say, the deadline passed and the brief, so crucial to The H Group's future, was left undone. In a spastic fit Tom assigned the brief to another lawyer who roughed out a draft in a day, and together they polished the copy and filed it. But the damage was done. The judge, none too happy with their tardiness, ruled against them. And in six month's time the case was lost.

So was Mel and Rita's marriage. They divorced just weeks later, and Rita, who was always the better lawyer (and by far the shrewder person) took Mel to the cleaner's. But the real victim of their split was The H Group: Had Tom acted on his hunch and questioned their status—and their work—sooner, the verdict may have worked in their favor.

The 5-15 Report

Every sponsor needs to be managed; the worse the sponsor, the more you'll need to manage him. Hence any tool that can help you is worth its salt, as is this, the *5-15 report*.

Unless your sponsor is stunted, the report should take him no more than five minutes to read and you no more than 15 minutes to write. Hence its name. In five sections it says the following:

1. How you made the firm money this week

2. How you saved the firm money this week

3. Any crises you thwarted

4. Any crises you handled

5. Things you need from the sponsor

Write this report on the same day each week. (Friday is good but Monday is better: On Monday you'll have the chief's full attention, as he won't be distracted by the weekend's revelries.) And be careful: Don't brag or toot your own horn. If there's nothing to write in any of the sections above, don't write anything. Don't pad your resume. And whatever you do, let no one know that you write this report. Make it a private missive between you and the project sponsor. This is your chance to show him your worth.

Constructive (Not Destructive) Confrontations

Conflict happens. There's no way to avoid it completely. (True, you can tone it down, and the tips in the section "The ABCs of Project Politics" will help, but you can never do away with it entirely.) It's simply what happens when you herd people together in an office, and put them on project teams: There's bound to be competing agendas and egos, and from time to time they'll clash.

Most conflicts are short; they result from harsh words or impatience or coffee spilled on your new pair of Pradas. But from time to time there are enduring conflicts, most often based on a personality clash. These conflicts sap energy from the office and can truly hinder the efforts of a team. They can stifle efficiency and destroy your peace of mind. They can make you miserable. And they can derail your projects with unrivaled ease. Hence these are conflicts that need resolution. These are also conflicts that need *mediation*.

Mediation is a way of resolving disputes, in which two warring parties meet with an impartial "judge" (the mediator) and try to work out their problems. It's not the mediator's job to determine who's right and wrong and punish someone as a result. Instead, it's his job to help the parties find compromise or common ground for their issues. It's a bit like marriage counseling: Both parties vent their complaints and then try to meet the other party halfway.

If you've got an enduring conflict with a colleague, the kind that's built on layers of resentment and that's lasted for months or even years, don't try to end it yourself. Ten to one, you'll just make it worse. You'll approach your "enemy" and start with a level head and calm voice, but your common history will overwhelm you and there's every chance that you'll end up at blows.

Instead, enlist the help of a mediator. The mediator should

- Get along with both you and your enemy.

- Have your respect, and your opponent's as well.

- Be truly neutral. He should have no stake in the outcome of this process.

- Have authority in the office. You can choose a mediator who's on the same level as you are in the food chain, but it's better to choose a bigger fish, the kind who can impose discipline if it comes to that.

- Be calm, rational, and not prone to anger. Choose someone who won't lose his cool, even if you do.

- Talk well. If you can, choose someone with a gift for language, the kind of person who knows how to persuade.

- Have tact. (No loudmouths need apply.)

Now approach the mediator and explain the nature of your conflict. (You may not have to explain it that much: If you have a conflict that's endured for months or more, then it's most likely grist for the office gossip mill.) Ask her to mediate between you and your colleague for a formal airing of grievances and an honest attempt at reconciliation.

Set a time and place for the meeting. For minor conflicts it's best to do it out of the office, even after hours. But for major conflicts you should use the office of your mediator. The formal nature of the place reminds everyone to be on his best behavior.

Next, view the meeting as an honest attempt to cut the Gordian Knot before you, and above all, be open to compromise. That said, don't be afraid to state your case forcefully—but professionally, too. Don't scream, shout, or whine; don't throw a block of Post-its at anyone. Just give your opinion of what's gone wrong in calm and measured tones, and don't hold back: This may be your last chance to air the dirty laundry that's fouling your work life.

Be willing to listen to complaints against you without being angered. You may not think they're right; you may not think they're fair; and that's fine. Say so. But don't lose your cool and above all, remember that you're not perfect. It takes two to tango, and in all honesty, it's likely that you've done something to anger your colleague just as he's done something to anger you.

Try to keep these points in mind:

- During the confrontation itself, avoid pop psychology. Shy away from lines like "I hear what you're saying" and "Let's dialogue about that." It makes people feel handled. It's phony. Just be honest and talk in your own voice.

- If you're nervous about what's about to happen, write down some talking points first. There's no reason you can't organize your presentation beforehand.

- Enter the meeting with a solution in hand. Don't just go to vent your feelings; after all, this ain't therapy. So plan an exit strategy *before* you get there, and make it detailed. Have some concrete steps in mind to improve your rapport with your nemesis. Suggest things you or your teams can do together, small but useful projects that you can accomplish without removing each other's jugular.

Of course, there are times when you'll need to mediate for members of your team, or at the very least arrange a mediation. As the team leader and project manager, it's your job to ensure harmony. (And if you can't do that, at the very least you can ensure the absence of clear and present conflict.) After all, it's your duty, just as much as writing the scope statement or fixing the budget.

It's also a duty you've never been trained for. When you got your PMP, you were schooled in the many ways to draft a schedule and assess risks and options. But you were never taught how to snuff out the fire of conflict and calm the angered soul on your team. Hence a few points to keep in mind when you're trying to resolve conflicts between team members:

- Never play favorites. You're the team leader and the exemplar of how to behave. If you act unjustly and privilege one team member over another, how can you expect your team to act any better, or show any maturity?

- If you have to, take yourself out of the loop. True, when team members fight it's your job to make peace. But that's *not* to say it's your job to mediate between them. In fact, sometimes it's best to identify the problem, talk with the warring parties about it, and arrange for someone else—a director, VP, and so on—to mediate the problem in a formal setting. That way you won't incur the resentment of one of your team members if you say the wrong thing in a mediation, and you'll have more time to spend on the core aspects of project management, not office politics.

- Remember the Godzilla Principle. As we said above, you need to nip small problems in the bud before they get too big (and eat Tokyo). As the team leader, you should be aware of conflicts when they start—that is, as they arise day by day. You should be savvy to team members' feelings and the internal dynamics of your group. That way you can see trouble brewing, and stop it *before* it becomes a problem so bad that it makes you want to scream.

Know Your Stakeholders

A stakeholder is anyone who has a legitimate interest in your project: your boss, your client, your sponsor, and so on. These are the people who will ultimately judge the success or failure of your project; how they see it, how they judge your performance, carries weight. In fact, it may be the key to your next promotion or simply your survival in your firm.

So invest the time it takes to know them well. At the start of a project meet with all key stakeholders one-on-one. Ask them how they define project success; what they expect to see for deliverables; what they believe are your largest risks; how they plan to interact with the team (Will they talk to them daily? Will they be at weekly meetings? Will they have any hands-on management roles? Will they observe and judge from afar?); what they need from you in terms of updates; and so on. Take notes. And offer your stakeholders your utter confidentiality; if you speak with them in private, they're likely to spill the beans on touchy subjects or key personnel. Of course, that's data you need in advance of your project so you can navigate the minefields they pose as the project unfolds.

Once you've met with your stakeholders, find a way to keep in touch with them weekly. This can be something basic, such as a weekly e-mail. Or for grandees, you can make it a point to have a weekly meeting—something brief but informative—just to touch base.

You may also want to assign a trusted deputy on the project team to personally mind important stakeholders. Choose someone with a head for politics and the ability to read moods and the occasional unspoken message. Make sure he gets along with the stakeholder in question and task him with caring for the stakeholder's needs.

Throughout the project you should actively solicit stakeholder feedback. This does *not* mean that you'll accept or (God forbid) implement everything they say; but at the very least you should ask them for their opinions, to make them feel valued and to get an outside view of your performance. And, while you won't take their every word as Gospel, be sure not to discount them either. When an important stakeholder requests a change in your project—a new deliverable or a change in process—accommodate when you can and be up front when you can't. People, by and large, prize honesty. They'd rather be told you can't help than to be led down a primrose path without results.

Last, make sure your stakeholders know one another, and know one another's needs. All too often conflicts arise when one stakeholder makes one demand that runs completely at odds to another stakeholder's needs. This leaves you, the PM (and team leader, and chief diplomat, and go-to guy) in the middle of two warring agendas. The best way to avoid a stay between the rock and the hard place is to ensure that your stakeholders understand—and over time, appreciate—one another's plans. How? Have a weekly or monthly meeting of key stakeholders in which only you and a trusted lieutenant meet them in a group and discuss the project's progress and ultimate goals. Then, if there are conflicts between stakeholders, they'll surface in the right place at the right time, and you can mediate between stakeholders to find a just conclusion to the crisis.

Last, a regular meeting of stakeholders helps you to avoid the tyranny of the majority stakeholder, in which one stakeholder—often the boss—overruns all others with his opinions. Given, a meeting of all stakeholders is no guarantee that one of them won't be able to monopolize the conversation. But it's easier to rein in a stakeholder when he's faced with other stakeholders' needs than when he's in isolation.

The Career-Killer Project: The Office Move

How's this for a scary fact: One-third of the project managers charged with handling an office move are no longer with their organization a year after the move is complete. They quit during the move itself, due to the stress of dealing with people (read: senior management) who want things done their way or the highway.

Another third of PMs are simply fired. They try to manage one of the worst jobs on earth, a highly political project, only to anger a VP whose new office won't have a corner window. And in the end, they become nothing but scapegoats.

Ouch.

So what should you do if your boss asks you to manage the office move?

Run. As fast as you can.

If that's too extreme, at least be smart about how you respond. Ask for some time to accept or decline the assignment. If you're given some time—and you're not inclined to manage the project—shop around the office to find someone who is. You may have to do some convincing. Appeal to their vanity (*This is an important project, which is why I thought of you*) or their corporate loyalty (*We're in a bind, and we really need someone to do this*). And if that doesn't work, then sell! Sell! Sell!

If you're able to find a flunkie to handle the move, then you've just salvaged your career. If not, then you'll need to get busy with the tips below.

Build the move team. You've gotta have some help. As soon as you can, start to organize your team. Be sure to get people from every department in your firm: Legal, Finance, IT, Operations, Sales, and so on. Why? Simple: The move will affect each of them in a different way, and you need to know how. (You can't fake it.) For instance, the folks in Accounting will pitch a fit if you move in the first 10 days of the month, while they're busy closing the books. Hence, as the PM, you'll have to work out a schedule that disturbs your key operations as little as possible.

Plan, plan, plan. Here's where your skills can shine. Approach the office move with the same tools you'd use on any other project. After assembling your team, have a project kickoff meeting and planning session. For a large move there are perhaps 1,000 tasks that you need to address. For a small one—say, for a small firm—there can be as few as 100 tasks. Either way, be sure you nail them down *before* you haul off the sofas. (Note that Microsoft Project has a template you can start with, which can be useful if you've never planned a move before.)

In the kickoff meeting, make assignments and note deadlines. Put them in writing and publish a detailed schedule to the project intranet. The same goes for a statement of scope and other project docs, such as the Pleasure and Displeasure List and the Responsibilities Matrix.

Time permitting—and you should make the time—have weekly status meetings to ensure you're keeping your schedule. As the move date gets closer, you may start to meet daily.

And keep in mind the following tips:

- Buy, borrow, or rent any special equipment you'll need in advance. (Book carts, gondolas, and file transporters come to mind.)

- Pay special care to certain equipment, such as computers and copy machines whose warranties may stipulate that specially qualified movers are needed.

- Make friends with your IT group. In fact, make *best* friends with your IT group. They're a vital part of your project. After the move you can make do with a missing table or box, but you can't exist without computers and phones.

- If there's a union where you work, watch out for union rules. Unions often have rules that govern office moves, and you'll need to respect them if you expect to pull your move off with success.

Build an inventory. When you move, everything—utterly every-thing—needs to be inventoried. The inventory is among your most important assets. It becomes the bedrock of your planning and bidding process.

A few handy tips for your inventory:

- Be sure to note those items that will be broken into sections, like a long conference table or a three-section credenza. That way you can mark and number each section, ensuring they'll all arrive at your destination.

- Take the inventory at night. You'll have access to all the rooms in your office, and you won't have as many interruptions.

- If you can, use a database and bar code scanners. If you do, you can sort the inventory by office, department, furniture type, disposition, and more.

Get the bids. When word hits the street that you're planning a move, get ready to man the phones. You'll be called by movers, contractors, office landscapers, phone companies, coffee service vendors, and more.

But the key is the office mover. For the most part, movers are regulated by state governments, and some governments dictate the daily and hourly rates they can charge. Others don't, so you'll have to do the grunt work yourself. Make some calls and get the names of five movers that handled moves for people you know (and hopefully trust). But, rather than invite the movers to bid, ask them to send you a bid package they've done in the past. They'll be happy to, as they'll feel it gives them an inside track on your job. And you'll be able to sift through each package, pick out their best points, and assemble them into your own. Thus you've got the upper hand in the bidding war.

Choose a mover. At the end of the day, the mover that gets your job has your corporate fate in their hands. The group you choose may not be the lowest bidder, but the one that gives the best service. And no matter how you choose them, be sure to rely on a rational, practical decision process, no matter how savvy their salesperson is. Remember, he'll rarely be with you in the trenches on moving day.

Inform the masses. Truly, the corporate grapevine is highly efficient—and shockingly accurate. When news of "The Move" leaks out, employees will know in a matter of minutes. As the PM you'll have to keep them informed (and in some cases, calm) for the duration of the project. A simple newsletter is often the best way to push out key dates and events. Q&A sessions are helpful as well. You can train your team members and the human resource people to handle them.

Move (finally). "M" day is here. Relax. After all, it's only your career that hangs in the balance.

It's best to move on a weekend. That way you won't disrupt the normal flow of business, and you'll have time to test your computers, phones, and networks before things start in earnest on Monday. On Friday, have your boss let everyone go at noon, since they'll have to come back on Sunday to unpack their stuff.

Then, take your team of 12 to 50 people, with half at the old office and half at the new one, and start to kick ass and take names. The move will proceed around the clock until finished, since night and weekend moves tend to avoid the useless delay of traffic.

By Sunday you should be done. On Monday, put coffee and donuts in every work space. You'd be surprised to know how many problems can be relieved with a mild caffeine and sugar fix. For other complaints, have a help desk to record and solve each issue.

Then, when you're done, take a vacation. We suggest Maui or Bali. And whatever you do, don't take your cell phone.

Chapter Five

The Perfect Meeting

Is there such a thing as the perfect meeting? You're damn right there is. It's short, sweet, and productive. It gets to the point, then gets you out the door. It's scheduled well in advance and it's never a hassle. And, as you may have guessed, it's pretty rare.

Project management, of course, depends on meetings like fish depend on water. So we'll give you a few hints on having the perfect meeting in this chapter, in the hope that you have one—or more than one: dozens—in the near future.

The Cost of Meetings

Read this section carefully. It reveals a disturbing truth about meetings.

Let's start with some facts. Meetings rarely have a hard cost—that is, a cash outlay you can easily track. But they're full of soft costs—back-end costs such as lost productivity, the cost of the conference room, the cost of the furniture, and so on. Soft costs are rarely accounted for, but they can break the bank.

Let's start with salaries, the largest soft cost in any meeting. Let's say you've got an EVP who makes $200,000 per year. His hourly wage, presuming he works 40 hours a week and takes a three-week vacation in June, is $100 per hour. That means it costs you $100 to waste an hour of his time in a meeting. Now let's say you've got a team whose average hourly wage is $50. A meeting with 10 members of your team costs you $500 per hour—and that's only for their salaries.

If you'd truly like to know the real cost of the meeting, you'll have to know the following:

- How much the room costs you (after all, you're paying rent on it)

- The cost of the furniture

- The cost of the meeting equipment, such as audio-visual gadgets, paper for the agendas, and so on

- The cost of uploading the minutes to the Intranet or sending them out by e-mail

- And worst, the cost of lost productivity

That last one—lost productivity—is nearly impossible to measure, but it's like rust on the bottom line. It corrodes. Let's say you've got a coder who's working on a fancy database. To get to the meeting, he's got to stop what he's doing, do a little prep work (say, read an agenda or review some notes), and then walk to the meeting itself. That's a total of 10 minutes' time. Then, when the meeting's over, he's got to go to the bathroom, stop at the water cooler, get back to his desk, get back into his frame of mind, and start his work again—another 15 minutes down the drain. That's 25 minutes in all.

Now multiply that by 10 members on your team and you've got 250 minutes of lost time, or roughly four man-hours. Are you with us? Because this next part is scary. Take that figure—four man-hours—and multiply it by the average salary of your team (we said $50 before). That's $200 you've wasted just to get people to and from the meeting!

And if that weren't bad enough, keep in mind that it takes some people up to half an hour to get to a meeting and half an hour to get back to their desks, or more if they have to fly or drive to the meeting place.

Get the picture? Even a short meeting can drain hundreds of bucks from the corporate coffers. So, if you're truly concerned about the cost of corporate meetings, get thee to the Web and point your browser to www.EffectiveMeetings.com. This neat little site has an electronic meeting cost tracker. A little tool that you can download for free, it lets you input the number of meeting attendees and their average annual salary, then computes your meeting costs minute by minute.

But, beyond the fiscal cost, meetings cost your team its morale. People hate meetings, period. They drain energy; they grate on team members' nerves. If you have too many of them, your team will get angry, flustered, and flummoxed—not an ideal way to get things done.

All that said, here are a few points on cutting the cost of your meetings.

First, you can eliminate half of your information meetings by simply posting the same information to your corporate network or your project intranet. And in case you haven't heard, there's a new invention called e-mail that serves the same purpose nicely.

Here's another thought: Have your team read updates or other meeting material *before* they attend the meeting itself. That way you won't have to waste your breath repeating them (the updates, that is, or whatever else you've asked your team to review) during precious meeting time. And for God's sake, if you've got stuff for people to read before a meeting, give it to them before the meeting—*way* before the meeting, say, two to three days in advance. Don't send it by e-mail an hour before and expect your team to have read it in full. There's just no way they can.

Third, talk fast. (Don't scoff. It's a simple rule that works.) People tend to ramble in meetings and you, for one, should not. This goes double if you're the team leader or meeting facilitator. Remember your high school English teacher's (rather good) advice: Be concise. People will love you for it.

Types of Meetings

How many kinds of meetings are there? Over a thousand, and we're going to list them all below. So kick back and take a Valium. You've got some reading to do.

Not.

There are really only two kinds of meetings: information and action meetings, and we'll describe them both with concision and brevity (in deference to your mental health).

Let's start with *information meetings*. These meetings are not designed to get things done or make decisions. They're simply meant to spread information, most often to your project team. These meetings are used for daily updates and project updates; standup meetings (discussed below) fall under this rubric as well.

Information meetings have little in the way of follow-up. There are rarely any minutes (often, these meetings are simply too short for minutes) and few action items to fulfill.

Action meetings, on the other hand, are a different kettle of fish. They're designed to get something done or make decisions. As opposed to information meetings, they're filled with give and take, arguments (polite ones, we hope), and highly interactive discussions. And they're always followed up by action item reports or meeting minutes, which you can post to the project intranet. (If you don't have one, e-mail will do, but do get one if you can: An intranet will quickly become the nervous system of your project, your one most useful tool. We'll discuss it at length in Chapter 6, "Awesome Technology.")

The only people who should attend action meetings are those who can help reach a consensus. Resist the urge to stock your meeting with people who do nothing to add to decisions but only fuel the debate. They'll make your meetings longer, more boring, and in the end, largely useless.

In fact, you can herd your action meeting attendees into three categories: *ATT* (*At the Tables*), *ITRs* (*In the Rooms*), and *OTPs* (*On the Phones*).

ATTs sit at the meeting table and actively engage in the debate. They're players. On the other hand, ITRs are not there to speak, but observe and absorb information. They're seated along the walls of the conference room and not the main table itself. When they have something to say—which is rare, and only when called upon—they rise, approach the table, and speak their peace. Then they return to their chairs on the sidelines. OTPs, of course, are listening by phone, and that brings a whole slew of problems into the fray. Often, the people at the table mumble, gesture, and don't speak loud enough—and clearly enough—to be heard by the OTPs. Consequence? OTPs are often shut out of most of the meeting, or, at the very least, annoyed by having to listen so hard just to follow its course.

If you're going to invite a person to attend your meeting by phone—especially if she's an important person—do the decent thing and invest in a good speakerphone. Don't use the one that came with your office phone, or the one on the phone in the conference room. Instead, spend the dollars to get a decent conference phone from a vendor like Nexus or Avaya. True, they ain't cheap (you can expect to pay $500–$1,000 for the equipment alone), but your OTPs will thank you. (If you're not sure where to get a good phone, point your web browser to www.hellodirect.com. You'll see more speakerphones than you can imagine.)

Parsing your team into ATTs, ITRs, and OTPs can make your meeting more efficient. Only those who should be talking will be talking, and that, by definition, keeps you from wasting time on idle comments and useless debate. But there's a problem in splitting your group into people who should sit at the table and people who sit by the walls—namely, how you do it. You need to do it with tact. Some people get ticked when you tell them to buck up, button their lips, and step back from the table. Like all of us, they have an ego, and their ego tells them they should be talking. What's more, you may have a burning desire to put someone important—say, a VP or director—against the wall to shut him up.

So what do you do? First, you bite the bullet and accept the fact of office politics (Chapter 4, "Surviving the Corporate Jungle," will help you with that). If you're going to segment your group for meetings, you'll have to make concessions to the office pecking order, and put some people at the table who, in truth, should be against the walls. And since there's only so much room at the table, you may have to put some people against the walls who should have a prime speaking position. It's just the way of the game.

We suggest you do it with care. If someone attacks you for being designated an ITR, take him aside and explain your dilemma. Tell him you only have so much time and you want the meeting to move quickly. That's your job. And in doing your job you have to make some hard decisions. This is merely one of them, not meant to irk or offend.

And if that fails to work, slap him upside the head.

Standup Meetings

This, in case you've never seen one, is a chair:

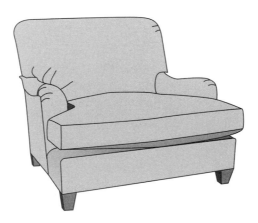

Not just any chair, of course. This is one helluva chair. With its rich, distressed leather, its soft cushions, its high plush back, this chair just begs to be sat in. This is a chair you can fall asleep in. This is a chair your butt will love. This chair, friends, is the enemy of your meetings.

And not just this chair. Any comfy chair is deadly to meetings. They encourage people in meetings to sit back, relax, and take their time. And the last thing you want people to do in a meeting is take their damn time.

What you really want, if you want your meetings to be short and sweet, is a meeting without chairs. A *standup meeting*. It's a brief, five- or ten-minute meeting in which no one sits. Typically, they stand in a circle and wait to bolt for the door—which is why the meeting is fast. No one can sit, relax, and take his time. It's simply harder to gab and gab for hours when you're on your feet (in heels, no less). (In fact, if you really want your meetings to fly by, make everyone wear heels. Men too.)

Because of the short nature of standup meetings, they're by and large informational. These are not meetings where you make a decision or sit and solve problems. In fact, most of the people who go to these meetings don't even speak: They come to listen. Trust us. If everyone starts opening his yap, these meetings will drag on and on, ad infinitum. So we suggest a simple rule for your next standup meeting: Let only your team members speak, or, if you have time to do this beforehand, let only those who've asked you to speak before the meeting do so.

In fact if you run these meetings right, they're not long enough for an agenda. And if there is an agenda—which is rare for a standup meeting—it's short: one, two, or three items at most.

Now let's talk about where, when, and how often you'll hold your standup meetings. It's wise to hold them in hallways, not in conference rooms; that way they'll end more quickly. There's just something about a conference room that makes people dither. Plus, if you hold your meetings in hallways, they can move from place to place, say, from one cubicle to another, or from one computer to another, as people show their work or touch on different subjects.

(Now, we know that you're a PM, a structured, ordered type who's been trained to get the most of conference rooms, and for people like you a loose meeting in the hall is about as appealing as a Sumo wrestler in a Speedo, but give it a chance. After a meeting or two where no one sits and you're done in five minutes flat, you'll be hooked.)

As for when, most standup meetings are held at the beginning of the day as status meetings or daily kickoff meetings, but every now and then, you may want to meet at the end of the day to review what's happened or set the plan for the following day. And those of you who qualify as meeting junkies can meet twice, once in the morning and once in the afternoon—but for Pete's sake, limit your meetings to five minutes apiece. Please. And do your best to avoid having meetings in the middle of the day; it makes it hard to schedule meetings with people outside the team. (There is, of course, one exception to this rule, and it goes like this: If you want a meeting to last x minutes, start it x minutes before lunch.)

How often should you have a standup meeting? As often as you need to and no more. Most meetings—in fact the vast majority—are needless; they're wasteful and useless. So only schedule a standup meeting when you have to do something you can't do by e-mail, memo, or the office grapevine. Of course, if you elect to have these meetings once a day, say, first thing in the morning, before your team gets to work in earnest, keep in mind that a short meeting can be the daily glue that binds your team together.

But a daily meeting that runs too long can also tick your team off. (We know; we've seen it happen.) So don't be afraid to play a game in your standup meetings: See how short you can make them—that is, see how efficient you can be. If you have to, use a timer and forcibly end the meeting when it goes off, no matter what's being said (unless it's the cure for cancer or something just as worthy). As your team evolves to the intuitive level (see Chapter 1, "Building the Killer Project Team"), count on your meetings to get shorter and shorter. If you can have a standup meeting in five minutes flat and still convey the entire day's tasks, then you're one hell of an organized team.

9 A.M., No Matter Who You Are

It's 9 A.M., and everyone—every last person, from the CEO to the men who clean the toilets—in a major hotel chain are about to do the same thing. They're about to take part in a standup meeting.

Why bother? Because it's not simply the way they get organized. Hands down, it's the way they maintain their world-renowned service in each of their 40 hotels across the globe. For 10 minutes every day, the whole company, *en masse*, thinks about the same issues.

Every morning at precisely 9 A.M., 30 of the chain's top brass gather for a 10-minute standup meeting in the hallway outside the office of the president at corporate headquarters. Then, within 24 hours, at every hotel from Montreal to Milan, the rest of the hotel chain's employees kick off their daily shifts with their own standup meetings. The meeting is split into three parts: First they cover the "topic of the week," such as this month's financials or the new hotel they're about to open in Nice. Next they review customer service basics. They end with an update on operational issues.

Since their hotels never close, 24/7/365, it's crucial for the chain to reinforce its corporate philosophy and continue to enhance its level of service. So these meetings—short, sweet and on point—are 10 minutes well spent.

Pre-Flight Checklists

Funny what a piece of paper can do, and what kind of havoc its absence can wreak. Here we mean agendas, those little sheets of paper that tell you what's up in a meeting. Every meeting has to have one; a meeting without one, except the very shortest, is just a recipe for disaster. And meetings *with* agendas are almost always taken more seriously by the team members who attend them. After all, when you receive an agenda it's an official invitation of sorts, and it carries more weight than a simple e-mail or an invitation by word of mouth. So if you don't have an agenda at your next meeting, take five minutes at the start of the meeting to write one. Consider it your pre-flight checklist. (Then, if you're so inclined, pass out those little bags of peanuts and tell people to buckle their seat belts.)

Here's a quick list of what to include in your agendas:

- The meeting's location. (Choose someplace easy to get to.)

- The start time and end time. (The latter is crucial; some agendas don't have end times, and they're bad agendas; they implicitly encourage meetings to go on and on.)

- The meeting's participants. (As a golden rule, invite as few people as possible, and the fewer the better—your meetings will end sooner. Just make sure you've got the right people there. There's nothing worse than calling a meeting and not having the people you really need to get something done.)

- Topics for discussion.

- The presenter for each topic.

- The time allotted for each topic. (Which should be sacrosanct; if you've allotted 10 minutes for your discussion of Jurassic fossils, spend 10 minutes on your discussion of Jurassic fossils, and no more—you'd be surprised how fast 10 minutes will turn into 20, and 20 minutes into 30 if you're not careful.)

- The meeting's scribe, if there is one. (We'll discuss this shortly.)

- Last but not least, the meeting leader.

Now, a few points on writing agendas. As banal is it may seem, it takes time to perfect the art of the agenda, so here's a rule or two to follow:

- An agenda need not be elaborate; in fact, the best agendas are simple. Write only what you need to, and leave all else out.

- Don't be a fool: Be smart with the amount of time you give each presenter. Remember that people are verbose by nature; they'll hem and haw and talk as long as they can, so don't cram too much into an hour's meeting. In fact, if you have only an hour to meet, schedule no more than 50 minutes of discussion. Thus you've got 10 minutes to spare (which you'll almost always use) and if you don't, you're done early—reason enough to rejoice.

- Rank items on the agenda by importance. Put the most urgent ones first, so you can get *to* them and *through* them. (For instance, that discussion of whether or not to replace the office coffee pot with a bottle of Jack can wait till the back end of the meeting—unless, of course, it's Monday, when you deal with this first.)

- For longer meetings, don't forget to include breaks. A good rule of thumb: Take a 10-minute break every hour to accommodate your team's weaker bladders.

- Distribute the agenda beforehand, at least by a day (and two is better). It's best to send it by e-mail or post it to the project intranet—after all, who needs another piece of paper on his desk?

- Be sure to ask people for feedback. You may have left something off or someone may want some time in the meeting.

- Make a list of offline discussion for later. For instance, if someone brings up a topic that's not germane to the current meeting, save it for an e-mail exchange, a discussion forum on your intranet, or a separate meeting altogether.

Remember, the hardest part of writing agendas is learning to follow them during your meetings. Don't be tempted to divert from your agenda for any reason at all. If you do, you'll find your meeting runs longer than it should, which is the first—and most cardinal—sin.

If someone brings up a point that's important but not urgent, one that's off the agenda but should still be discussed, save it for after the meeting. Discuss it by e-mail, or use a discussion board on your project intranet. And, if the topic is truly vital, schedule a new meeting devoted entirely to it.

The Loudmouth

We love a good loudmouth. Not a *real* loudmouth, mind you, the kind that irks and annoys. The loudmouth we love is highly respected, a keen diplomat, and a master talker: He's a *meeting facilitator*.

Frankly, every good meeting needs one. Much like a meeting without an agenda, a meeting without a loudmouth is a recipe for disaster—too many people talk at once, there's no order, and things get left undone. It's a bloody mess.

So who should the loudmouth be? *Not the boss.* Dear God, not the boss: They tend to be autocrats who talk half the time and lead meetings astray. It's just the nature of the beast. What's more, people tend to parrot the boss, and the only thing that does is make for bad chatter. So it's better to have a professional loudmouth at the head of your meetings, to run them efficiently. People are more at ease, more open, and more willing to share their opinions.

That said, who should the loudmouth be? He (or she) should be a trained meeting leader, someone who knows how to focus the room's energy and keep it moving; someone who knows how to parcel out time politely and keep people on track. The loudmouth needs to be a unique blend of cheerleader and referee: a cheerleader because he gets people involved, gets their attention, keeps them excited, and asks them questions; a referee because he moderates and makes sure that any conflicts that arise in the meeting are fully resolved.

Loudmouths need to be good talkers by nature. Theirs is not a role for the shy or demure among us. And loudmouths need to be good diplomats. Theirs is not a role for the crude or the pushy either. What they need to be, in essence, is a catalyst: They stimulate discussion; they make ideas flow. And they're a bit of a disciplinarian as well: Their job is to keep track of the agenda and make sure it's followed. (Otherwise put, a good catalyst knows when to massage the meeting and when to crack the whip.)

Anything else? You bet. Loudmouths determine when the group is ready to make a decision, at which point they draw all conversation to a close and call for the decision to be made. Loudmouths moderate. They let someone finish a point or get back to him if he's been cut off. And loud-mouths relate. They relate one person's thoughts to another's, creating synergy as they go.

Two last notes on loudmouths before we move on to the next topic. First, the loudmouth should be positioned at the head of the table or its focal point. If the tables are in a U formation, as they should be for a large meeting, he should be at the open end of the U, and should be standing, walking, and talking, the better to direct and command the meeting.

And last, bear in mind that you can hire an expert loudmouth for your next big meeting. Believe it or not, there are people who do this full-time, and you can find them on the Web at www.facilitators.com. Of course, as a PM and talented chicken herder, you'll be the loudmouth in most of your meetings, and that's just fine. Just be sure to do the job with care, since all eyes are on you.

The Scribe

*Scribes…*They're as old as antiquity, as old as writing itself. In ancient Egypt, scribes lined the walls of the pharaohs' tombs with words that few people could read (but many, if not most, feared). In medieval times they designed wonderous books that informed priest and penitent alike. Today they fill whiteboard on whiteboard with notes in modern meetings.

Scribes (also called note-takers or minute-takers) are neutral parties in any meeting. They capture ideas, decisions, and such on a whiteboard or flipchart, or by taking notes to pass around later. They write the minutes if there are minutes to write; they work up action items and send them out to the team.

You can train an assistant to fill the role of the scribe with relative ease. After all, it's not rocket science; it's merely writing. Any literate soul will do. Just put him at the front of the room or behind the meeting leader; he'll use a whiteboard or large flipchart to write up ideas as they come into being. It keeps the meeting on track and makes it more concrete.

One last thought: If you're short an assistant to act as the scribe, you can pass the duties from one team member to the other. Or you can assign the scribe's duties to a person who always skips your meetings. By giving him (busy) work, it's a good way to make him show up.

Rules of the Road

Hint: It's a bad sign if your meeting erupts into name calling and food fights. That's why it's wise to have *rules of the road* to go by. These are rules for how the team plans to conduct itself during the entire project, but in meetings in particular. Look at them as a way to keep the boys and girls in the sandbox happy.

Here's how to make them. At the start of your project—the kickoff meeting's a good time—gather your team and have them decide on rules of common conduct and courtesy. The group should decide as a whole; that means a unanimous vote. Then, once you've got the rules in place, stick them in the project library and post them to the project intranet.

Here's an example or two you can use:

- Respect the airtime. Don't interrupt; don't shout anyone down.

- Have a clock. Use the clock. Get out of meetings on time.

- Timeouts are fine. Everyone needs a break now and then, and it's best to grab one when things get heated.

- Never take cheap shots. Enough said.

- Own what's yours. If you've made a mistake, admit it. If you're the reason for a success, say it—but don't flaunt it. (Never, ever flaunt it: It's poor taste.)

- Avoid side conversations. This is not the fourth grade and we're not passing notes, either.

- Represent all the interests in the room. Let everyone speak—even those with unpopular opinions. (Often it's the least popular opinion that's right.)

- Commit to starting and ending the meeting on time. Make everyone respect a common schedule.

- Never leave a meeting without action items or, at the very least, a brief summary of what you did or what you said. Otherwise you've wasted your time.

Meetings: Make 'Em Fun

Not every meeting need be dull. For instance, you can hire strippers to liven them up. (Sorry. You should keep the strippers for the firm's Christmas party; be sure to get one for the boss.)

The truth is, we're asked to attend so many damn meetings that most of us do whatever we can to get out of them—we fake conflicts, we fake coronaries, we pretend we're not needed, and more. But if you can make your meetings fun—or at the very least enjoyable—you've got a better shot at getting stuff done, and getting stuff done is the name of the game. So remember these points and use them at your leisure:

- Feed people. They always flock to free food.

- Don't just talk. Include some activities like role-playing games, live demos of new products, and more. The more you can do that's not merely verbal, the better your meeting will be. (Just be careful of hotkey, stupid games that no one but the meeting planner likes. At all times, remember that you're dealing with adults, and they rightly hate to be treated like children.)

- In real estate, it's location, location, location. Same with meetings. Take 'em outside and enjoy the open air. Who likes to work under fluorescent lights, anyway?

- Charge people to speak. Give everyone at your meeting five pennies, and whenever one of them speaks, charge him a penny. This keeps two or three people (and you know who you are) from dominating the conversation.

- Remember to have frequent breaks. Once every hour is good.

- Run contests. Give away something worth winning.

- Be funny. A little laughter goes a long way.

Springtime

A Cincinnati winter can be dreadful. By its very nature, Ohio attracts an undue amount of snow, often coming in massive waves as storms pass through. So by the time that spring arrives, everyone's got the urge to get outside the office and get rid of the shackles of cubicles and wan fluorescent lights.

In 2004, Heather D., the IT director at a chain of hardware stores in Cincinnati, was also the team leader for the deployment of a new system-wide computer platform for her company. It was crushing work, the kind that kept her bent over her desk for days at a time, the kind that made the eyes bleary and the head sore. She despised it, and longed for the project's completion.

Then, early one Monday, while preparing for the day's project status meeting, she glanced out the window and caught sight of the picnic tables and chairs on the grass outside her office. "Why not?" she thought. "It's a decent day. Let's take this meeting outside."

Why not, indeed. It was to be a short meeting with no PowerPoint presentations or other digital wizardry, so there was no reason to coop yourself up in a dark room with shades drawn. And once they were outside in the clean spring air, her team began to perk up, showing a vitality that had been lost in the last several months.

As a result, Heather changed the location of every second meeting to the picnic tables, keeping the conference room for meetings in between. The fresh air gave life to her meetings and made the dull, driving work less crushing on the brain. ✐

Meeting Glitches

Ain't nothing perfect, and meetings, as we all know, are no exception. Here are some cures for some common meeting ailments.

Meeting skippers Every project has one or more meeting skippers. The best thing to do is to assign the skipper a topic or task for the next meeting, where he's required to bring information or make a brief presentation. You can also make him the scribe (see above for a nifty description). Here's the point: Do whatever you can to ensure his physical presence at your next get-together. If that means giving him work, so be it. It's his fault he skipped in the first place.

Of course, if you've got several people who skip, then take the hint: They may be on to something. Your meetings could be too long or simply irrelevant. (Remember that most meetings are, and most people attend only because they have to.) If that's the case, search your soul and see if your meetings really serve a purpose. If you have doubts, ask around. People will tell you the truth; they may even delight in it, much to your dismay.

Latecomers Slowpokes do more than disrupt the meeting. They waste time, since you have to go back and rehash what you already covered. So next time put a note on the agenda: Latecomers will be hanged. If that's too direct for your style, you can always say that you appreciate promptness, and that, for the sake of time and efficiency, you won't repeat what's already been said for those who come tardy.

If it's the boss who's late—say she's always late by 10 minutes—sit down and talk with her: A direct approach is often the best, especially when the problem's habitual. You might find out that your boss has good reason to be late (more than merely arrogance, that is). She may have a conference call or some other obligation that always runs over, one that's scheduled just before your meeting. If that's the case, shift the official start of the meeting back by a quarter-hour.

Sly talkers Sly talkers are those people who insist on talking during meetings (often in sly whispers or little side chats). We recommend the use of a whip to keep these people in line. A cattle prod will do nicely as well. Use it sparingly. Apart from that, you can always call attention to these members of your team and ask them if they'd like to share with the group. But do so with care: Don't make yourself sound like a high school teacher (and a bad one at that). We're all grown-ups; treat even your ruder team members with a dollop of respect.

If the problem is habitual, try a seating chart for the meeting—and break up your Chatty Cathys. Or, if the problem persists, try to involve them in the main line of conversation by asking them questions (*What's your opinion about what Balthazar just said?*) If the side conversation is especially rude, you can always shut up and stare at the offenders ... they're bound to notice and zip it up.

Arguments Some people just love to argue. Once again we recommend the use of a whip or cattle prod to keep these people in line. That aside, you can let the offender run his mouth for a while. Sooner or later (and most likely sooner), he'll tick off the group, and like vultures descending on carrion, they'll finish him off for you.

There's also the direct approach: Simply turn to the offender and tell him you don't think his line of conversation is productive. Then quickly turn to another team member and ask him a direct question to keep the conversation moving forward (dead air is a danger in meetings).

Of course, if you've got a truly functional team, the kind that knows and trusts each other, a dust-up now and then can be a good thing. Some of the best ideas come from friendly conflicts, and what project can't use its share of really good ideas?

Dominators Dominators are people who dominate the discussion—often with nothing to say. Sadly, it's often the boss or someone who's simply more senior than you are, and when it happens, your team, like so many beaten soldiers, just sit back and give up the floor. In this case it's your job as the PM or facilitator to ask other team members pointed questions and draw them into the discussion. Since you can't bind and gag the boss (much as you'd like to), make it a point of not making eye contact with him. It makes it harder for him to steer the discussion.

The shy type The reverse of the dominator is the shy type who lacks self-confidence, perhaps a new recruit or some other newbie. They've often got fresh ideas, but they're merely unwilling to share. If this is the case, it's the responsibility of the PM or facilitator to get them to do that, to ask them questions and draw them into the discussion.

The Ultimate Waste of Time

Tuesday morning, 10 A.M., and the office was quiet. The phones were calm (a rare delight at this Newark biotech firm), the morning talkers had already come and gone, and Keith H., a Ph.D. and research VP, had cleared his inbox of all the e-mail that swamped it the night before.

He was ready. Before him on his teak desk (a trophy he brought back from a vacation to Thailand) lay the firm's draft FDA filing for Doxinil, its new cancer drug. It was nine years in development, and the firm's application to the FDA, crucial by any measure, was a colossal moment for this company. They'd spent upwards of $90 million in research and staked the bulk of their future earnings on this one little pill.

So needless to say, Keith was in a near trancelike state of concentration. For the last week he'd been writing, re-writing, and rewriting again, drafting the filing to a state of near perfection. And today was the last day: Another hour, and he'd be done. A neurotic, a perfectionist, and a fine scientist, Keith took no less pride in this memo than a poet would in his verse.

Then he heard it. It came over the intercom like a cold breeze:

Your attention please. The staff meeting will begin in five minutes in the conference room. All employees must attend.

The staff meeting? What staff meeting? Keith checked the group schedule in Outlook and saw that nothing was there; the 10 A.M. slot was empty. But he knew all too well what he was in for. The president, a brilliant, manic, slightly lunatic man with a Himalayan ego, had called the meeting on a whim, with no advance notice, and frankly, no reason save his own amusement.

These meetings were toxic. One- and two-hour affairs, they were little but ragtag collections of workers forced to endure longish, dull reports on matters of no substance. Then, like children, they were made to stand before the crowd and state their plans for the next day—plans that were delayed or even derailed by a useless meeting that was wholly resented.

And it was costly, too: Staff meetings were 30 to 40 people strong, depending on who was in the office when they were called. Most of those present were directors, VPs, and senior VPs, men and women who made hundreds of thousands per year. An hour of their time, much less two, could buy dinner for three at Lutece.

So Keith put away his work—not for the first time, of course—grabbed a notebook, and trudged down the hall. His morning was shot, his focus destroyed, and his anger, often fierce, was bubbling just below the surface of his skin. Yet another day wrecked by a useless meeting.

A year later, Doxinil was denied by the FDA, and the firm, low on cash and even lower on morale, went under.

Time Wasters

The best way to keep from wasting time is knowing how time is wasted. With that in mind, we've assembled a few meeting time wasters below:

- Start late. In fact, the later the better. There's no better way to waste time than to give it up at the start of your meeting.

- If you'd like to be a world-class time waster, start without an agenda. Better yet, hide the agenda and ask people to search for it.

- Better still, try two agendas, say, from two strong-willed souls who'd like to use your meeting to promote their own initiatives.

- Don't set a meeting end time. The meeting will drag on and on *ad infinitum*. You'll have gray hair (or more gray hair, or simply no hair) by the time it's finished.

- Meet without a loudmouth present. Remember that meeting facilitators serve to grease the meeting's wheels. Without one, your meeting will be slow and rusty.

- Forget to schedule breaks. If you do, you'll have one member of your team out of the room almost constantly, getting coffee, going to the bathroom, and more. Then you'll have to repeat what you said when he returns.

Of course, sometimes meetings themselves are the worst time wasters of all. Having too many of them, meeting on useless topics, or calling too many people to your meetings (and thus making them too long) is simply a killer. It eats through time like a horde of locusts. And there will always be people who speak, think, and act with so much sloth that merely having them present in meetings can grind things to a halt. Sadly, there are precious few ways to deal with these snails. You could offer them espresso (three or four cups) before a meeting starts, or you could simply not invite them to your meetings. If you're in a bind and you *have* to invite them (if, say, your boss is a slow talker, and you can't politely tell him not to come to your next project review), then do whatever you can to limit their input.

WebEx: Care To Meet Without Meeting?

Sometimes there's no way to have a meeting. One of the people you need is stuck in Chicago, another in New York, and yet a third in Des Moines. And to make things worse, you're in Houston. You could make a conference call, but this meeting is just too important to do by phone. So, you tell Mike in Chicago, Mark in New York, and Matt in Des Moines to hop on a plane and get here by Friday. All's well and good, till Friday comes and Matt fails to show. You call his office, but they tell you he left this morning—for the airport, no less. You call the airline and they tell you his flight came in three hours ago.

What's up? Matt, poor soul, made it to Houston, but made the mistake of using a shady cab service to get to your office. They dropped him off on the wrong side of town and Matt, in his three-piece suit with Florsheims and a fancy notebook case, was quickly mugged. (Too bad that your client list—with all your sales data—was on his computer.) He walked to three phones before he found one that worked, and when he tried to call your office collect, not having so much as a dime to his name, your receptionist, a temp, turned down the call.

Names changed, this is a true story. The meeting never happened, of course, and hapless Matt, who may have had the Worst Day in Tarnation, got delayed six hours on his flight back to Des Moines.

Now, you may not have to take muggers into account when planning your next meeting, but you do have to deal with shoddy airlines, acts of God, and other delays when flying people in from out of town. And besides, airfare ain't cheap, and neither are hotels.

Enter *WebEx* (www.WebEx.com). It's a website that delivers online meetings to firms of any size. Using it, you can share slides, memos, letters, spreadsheets, video, and more in real time, using nothing more than your *web browser*. (For those of you not sure of that term, it means your copy of Internet Explorer or Netscape Navigator, the software you use to surf the Web.) Any member of your meeting—and you can have as few as two or as many as hundreds—can mark up the files on screen as you talk by speakerphone or watch one another by video. You can also record your meetings and save them for later review, a boon for people who can't be there. And all this can be done from your desk, without having to move an inch from your office.

All you need is a decent computer, a broadband connection to the Internet, a telephone, and, if you plan to use video, a small camera perched atop your monitor. (You can buy the camera for less than $200. Point your browser to www.webcamstore.com to browse.)

Think of what you can accomplish. You can

- Look at new products.

- Show PowerPoint slides.

- Review and finalize contracts.

- Edit documents, or write them from scratch, with complete team input.

- Have Q&A sessions.

- Work out a budget.

- Train people on software, hardware, or PM techniques.

- Update your team on process changes or compliance issues.

- Hold team meetings with people in all corners of the globe.

And more, all without leaving your desk. WebEx is reasonably priced—it comes in several plans you can tailor to your business—and better yet, you can get a free demo (and a free trial) of the service by pointing your browser to www.WebEx.com. True, it takes some time to get your team used to meeting in cyberspace, but once they do, the payoff is worth it: No more cramped seats on airplanes. No more airplane food. No more rushing through airports. And for the luckless among us, no more muggings—reason enough to rejoice.

When to Schedule the 10 A.M. Meeting

You schedule the 10 A.M. meeting at 10 A.M., right?

Wrong. People expect to meet at 10 A.M., 12 P.M. and at other standard times, right on the hour or the half-hour. It's simply how we do business. And we've been doing it this way for since Adam bit the apple.

But when you schedule a 10 A.M. meeting (or a 1 P.M. meeting, or a 2 P.M. meeting), do people show up on time? Some of them do, and if you're lucky, maybe most of them do, but, according to Murphy's Law, you'll always have a straggler or two who comes in late—five minutes late, 10 minutes late, or even more. You'll have to stop the meeting to acknowledge him, or worse, go back and repeat what's been said. It wastes time, and it ticks people off. (And if you think this is a blunt way of putting it, or of looking at office life in general, remember O'Toole's Corollary to Murphy's Law: Murphy was an optimist.)

We've hit on a clever answer that works for these latecomers: Schedule the meeting for 9:54. Or 10:06. Or something similar. And when you distribute the agenda, include this language at the very top:

*This meeting will start exactly on time. Please be **extremely** prompt.*

When your team gets the agenda, they may think you're a little bit daft. (They may be right, but that's another matter.) They may call or e-mail you and ask about your choice of start times. Simply ignore them. What matters is this: An odd start time, one that's completely non-standard, will stick in their heads. They'll wonder, "Why then?" And as the meeting draws near, they'll look at their clocks and show up exactly on time—or better yet, a bit early. They'll do so in confusion; they'll wonder—maybe out loud—why you've chosen an odd time to start your meeting. But they'll be there, and that's what counts.

Chapter 6

Awesome Technology

There are two kinds of people in this world: Those who take to technology like a fish to water, and those who fear it like Jaws. (We'll deal with the second group later, in the section "Dealing with Luddites.")

For now, we'll assume you're somewhere between the two: a smart project manager who takes his technology in moderation. Computers neither delight nor scare you, but you've learned how to use them with a level of skill that lets you survive, if not quite flourish, in today's wickedly wired world.

Hence this chapter on awesome technology. Tamed and trained, computers can make your life simpler. More important, they can make your projects work better. It's just a matter of knowing how, and below we'll show you.

The Power of Project Intranets

If that word—*intranet*—sounds odd to your ears, we'll give you a definition: An intranet is simply an internal website that only you and your team have access to. It's *hosted* (that is, stored and served from a computer) inside your office and guarded by passwords or other protection schemes.

What's the first use of your intranet? Storing documents, of course, the same as your project library (but in electronic form). You can store documents securely with the knowledge that only those who are supposed to see them will. What's more, a well designed intranet will let you store your documents in versions, so you can see who's been using them, what changes they've made, and where things are at with each. You can order your files by department, by category, by project, by author, or any combination thereof. And a search function will let you locate docs by title, keyword, creation date, file size, file type, author, and more.

Think of just a few of the documents your intranet can host:

- Project charter

- Project plan

- Communication plan

- Stoplight charts, sorted by date

- Responsibilities matrix

- RFCs (requests for clarification), sorted by date

- Statement of work

- Statement of scope with all versions

- Status reports, sorted by week, project, or author

- Employee handbook

- Design specs and revisions

- Contracts with vendors and clients

- Meeting agendas, sorted by date, topic, or both

- Meeting minutes, sorted by date, topic, or both

- Policies and procedures

- Art library (with logos, product shots, etc.)

- Project budgets

And more. But using an intranet to store documents is only part of the picture. With the right programming, a project intranet can be a far more useful tool that includes

Online calendar Use this portion of your intranet to manage group schedules, appointments, events, deadlines, milestones, and functions. Well-designed calendars feature automatic reminders that get e-mailed to all meeting participants, the ability to attach documents or notes to entries on the calendar, the ability to compensate for time zone changes, a crisp printable format, and, for the best of the best, the ability to synchronize with Palm and Microsoft CE gadgets (such as Hewlett-Packard's iPAQ).

Task manager Use this section of your intranet to assign tasks to your project team and then view the status and progress of those tasks while they're in progress. Like the online calendar, the task manager should be able to synchronize with Palm and Windows CE tools. Good task lists will let you sort entries by owner, date assigned, date due, progress, and more, as well as send e-mail reminders to task owners as a due date nears.

Contact list Are you tired of searching your Rolodex for an important contact, only to find you don't have it, and that it's in the files of a colleague who's (in)conveniently out of the office when you need him? True, tools like Microsoft Outlook can let you store contacts and view and sort them with ease, as well as print and send them by e-mail. But in order to share those contacts, everyone in your firm has to have Outlook; what's more, it must be configured for shared access. Storing the contacts on a shared intranet, providing you have one, is a better solution. (Hint: When you team up with your IT group to design your intranet, ask them to include a way to attach photos to contact data.

That way, new team members can look at the photos and get to know the team and its major contacts.) Use your contact list to share data on team members, vendors, clients, partners, sponsors, and more. And once again, in tandem with the calendar and task manager, your contact list should synch with your Palm Pilot, BlackBerry, or other hand-held. (As you'll see later in this chapter, some commercial intranet products even let you access your contacts list from your mobile phone.)

Announcements How many times have you called a meeting just to share a set of announcements with your team, or sent those announcements out by e-mail? More times than you can count, we bet. But calling meetings simply to share information—and brief information especially—can be a useless time-waster. And sending the same information by e-mail adds one more piece of e-mail for people to open, read, and file or discard. What's more, if you have a large project team—say, dozens or even hundreds of members—that single e-mail you send is duplicated dozens or hundreds of times and ultimately clogs your servers with needless storage. Better to post those announcements to the homepage of your intranet, where users can read them every morning when they log on. Of course, to do that you'll need to get your team in the habit of checking the intranet daily—but with some prodding and poking you'll get even the most diehard of non-compliers to get with the program.

Opinion polls We live in a world driven—and riven—by polls. Our leaders (or perhaps we should merely say our politicians?) use them to gauge the public's stance on everything from the nation's defense to the state of the economy. And while polls and politics can be a toxic match, polling your team to get its opinion on important issues can be one hell of a useful tool for the PM who's eager to take his colleagues' pulse. You can use opinion polls to understand what your team is thinking—indeed, even *how* they think—or build consensus for new products. How? Take a poll on that new design prototype, for instance, or ask your team where they'd like to hold the Christmas party. Good poll software will let each team member vote his preference then collate the data and spit the results back in an easy-to-read, graphic format, complete with charts. (And truly good software will even show you the results in real time, as team members are voting.) Curious? Point your browser to www.pollmonkey.com or www.xigla.com for a deeper look.

Discussion forums We've all seen these on the Web, on everything from Latvian politics to recipes for sugar snap peas. Have you ever thought of using one for your project? A forum can let your team share thoughts on crucial issues (and minor ones, too) in a way that's saved and archived for later use, so someone who's missed the chat due to illness or travel or simply a busy schedule can still catch up. (A forum also leaves an audit trail in case you ever need one.) You can use forums as a suggestion box, a way to brainstorm and discuss policies, or even as a novel way to write and review status reports. If you really beg your IT group they'll even build you a forum that lets you search entries and attach documents to specific *threads* (threads are topics of discussion).

Custom apps The database: It's the granddaddy of intranet apps. With a database, you can use your intranet for everything from asset inventory to sales leads, event management to expense reports, resource schedules to large-scale contact lists. If you're an independent PM who works for clients on contract, you can use a database to enter time and billing info for your entire team, and have the system automatically tally and print your clients' bills. You can sort and collate your best practices in a system that lets them be searched on the fly. In short, there's nothing you *can't* do with a database shared over an intranet. It could be your team's most important tool.

The home page Last but not least, you can build a custom home page for your intranet, something with more than merely a corporate logo and color scheme. You can load it up with links to websites your team commonly needs, announcements of the sort discussed above, frequent document downloads (such as templates for expense reports, weekly and monthly status reports, meeting minutes, and the like), a web search feature (they're easy to build and sites like Google and Yahoo! let you use their engines for a small fee), news feeds for your industry or disciplines, company stock quotes, and more.

And these, of course, are only some of the ways to use your intranet. With time, you'll surely find other uses based on your business and the needs of your projects.

But what if you're in a small firm or you work solo, and there's no full-time group of webheads and techies to build, run, and support your intranet? No problem. You can rent one for as little as 50 bucks a month from sites like Intranets.com (www.intranets.com). In fact, even firms with massive IT staffs use Intranets.com and others like it to build simple intranets on the fly; they're full-featured (they have all the features mentioned above, and more), easy to build (you can build one in less than half an hour), easy to use (anyone who can use a website can use an intranet), and, perhaps best of all, backed up daily for total data security. (If you worry about prying eyes taking at peek at your data, don't. Intranet vendors often have a humdinger of a network security system.)

In fact, it may be simpler and cheaper to rent an intranet than to build it from the ground up. Intranets you rent or buy are often well conceived and built. Consider, for instance, this interface for the task manager from Intranets.com:

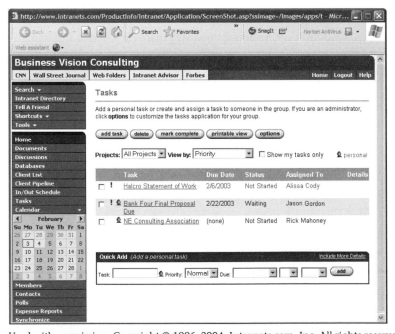

Used with permission. Copyright © 1996–2004, Intranets.com, Inc. All rights reserved.

It's clean, clear, and easy to use. To add a task you simply click the Add Task button in the top portion of the screen and follow the prompts, assigning a due date, team member, and details to the item. Tasks are shown in the middle of the screen and ordered by due date.

Still not convinced? Have a look at the home page for this intranet from Intranets.com:

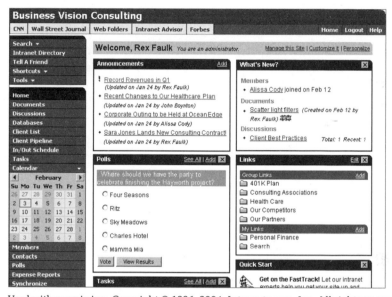

As you can see, it's just like using a website. Links are listed at the top and on the left-hand side of the screen. The rest of the screen is divvied up between boxes of content: Here, they're for announcements, polls, a What's New? section, group links to other websites, and more. Note how easy the poll is to use: Simply enter your choice and click Vote.

And if ease of use is not a good enough reason to build an intranet for your project team, consider this: Intranets save bundles of money in the long run. The savings on paper alone can be huge if your team is large. Instead of making three dozen copies of your last meeting's minutes and putting a copy on everyone's desk, you simply post the document to your intranet, where users can download and read it at their leisure.

And last, intranets vastly increase your team's production. If nothing else they save time—and time, in a project, is always your most precious asset. But even more, they let you communicate faster and better with your team, they solve the problem of multiple platforms in the enterprise (intranets can be used by people with Macs, Unix, IBM, and just about any other machine), and they give you a single, central tool to run an entire project, no matter how large it is.

Truly, what more could you ask for?

....

Hack Attack

It was, as projects go, one hell of a project. The intranet at Levitz & Sons, a firm that published textbooks for Texas schools (and whose name we've changed for privacy), took nearly a year to plan and execute. And it was worth it. It was the Aston Martin of intranets, with calendars, task lists, contacts, discussion forums, three database systems (one for expense reports, one for project updates, and one for revisions to books in progress), and a built-in video conference uplink so the firm's two offices, one in Houston and one in Austin, could keep in touch and keep it together.

It also had a document library with every page of every book the firm had ever published, and every page of every book the firm was going to publish. What it didn't have, as the PM in charge of the project, Lena M., would later realize to her chagrin, was an airtight security package.

On a Monday in November when Lena returned to the office after a long weekend, she set down her purse, kicked back her chair, and turned her computer on. Within a minute she was logging on to the intranet to check the daily announcements, when, to her shock and horror, she read this on the intranet's homepage in 24-point text:

"Wake up, friends! L & S management is raiding your retirement fund. Click here for proof."

She clicked.

She gasped. Someone had published reams and reams of the firm's accounting data—balance sheets, profit and loss reports, account statements, audit trails, and more—to her prized intranet. And chief among the exhibits was a spreadsheet that showed dozens of withdrawals from the firm's fat pension plan.

It took a week to sort out the details. When a forensic hacker was hired to vet the intranet and the firm's network for intrusions, he discovered that a former employee—a bookkeeper they'd recently fired—had used his former username and password to gain remote access to the system, raid the accounting folders, and publish the data he found to the intranet.

The moral of the story is simple. Keep your intranet safe. Use a *firewall*, passwords, and any other defense your IT group suggests. Lena M. was badly embarrassed by the hack (so bad she took a brief leave of absence), and, upon her return, was fired for negligence.

The Reach and Use of Project Extranets

What in God's name is an *extranet*? If nothing else it's a term you can wow your colleagues with at the water cooler.

Above, we said an intranet is simply an internal website that only you and your team can see. Well, an extranet is just a secured website that can only be seen by you, your team, and certain people *outside* your company who've been granted access with a username and password.

While intranets are used to share internal documents with your team, extranets are used to share docs and data and communicate with people outside your firm such as sponsors, clients, vendors, stakeholders, or share-holders. The most famous example of an extranet (though one that doesn't need a username and password to access) is the FedEx tracking site at www.FedEx.com. Using the extranet, you can enter your package number and other details to locate any package still in their system.

Of course, most extranets are far less awesome. They're simply private websites where a company communicates with its clients, vendors, share-holders, and so on. And much like an intranet, they're powerful tools for project management.

How? Think of an extranet as a reporting tool for use with anyone involved on your project but not directly on your project team. For example, you might want your sponsors and executives to have a calendar of project milestones, so they have a broad (but not too detailed) knowledge of your project's time structure. You could write that up in Microsoft Word, print out a dozen copies, and send it by snail mail, where it will be lost in the heaps of paper on your readers' desks; you could attach the file to an e-mail and send it out that way, where it becomes one of five dozen e-mails your read-ers will get in an hour; or you could post the document to your project extranet, where users can log on and read it at their leisure (and no doubt be impressed by your savvy technology).

Of course, a calendar is but one of the many things you can do on an extranet. Consider these:

Project docs You can share your important project documents with clients, sponsors, executives, stakeholders, and the like. These, of course, are the documents you want them to see, such as contracts, the statement of scope, and stoplight charts. Internal working documents, such as meeting minutes or memos, should be stored on your intranet.

Team bios Often your clients or sponsors don't get to know your team in any depth. They simply can't: They're not in your office and they tend to deal with a single point of contact (namely you, the PM) to get information. But your team is a prime selling point on any project, especially if you've built it with care. An extranet is a great place to post your team's bios and resumes, along with photos of each team member, for clients, sponsors, and others to browse. (This is *not* information you want on your public website, where it will quickly become bait for headhunters; but it *is* something you want your outside people to see.)

Collaterals Put your firm's brochures, sell sheets, and other collateral materials on your extranet. Just make sure they've been specially designed for on-screen viewing. Or, as an alternative, use *PDFs* (Adobe's Portable Document Format files) that users can download and print.

Legal docs If your project involves a lawsuit, you can post briefs, decisions, and other legal docs on your extranet. In litigation the cost of messengers often runs to thousands (if not tens of thousands) of dollars, and messengers take hours or even days to deliver important documents. True, you can send those documents by e-mail, but e-mail is inherently unsecured, and not the best way to pass confidential papers back and forth between parties. A secured extranet is.

Product designs If building a new product is the name of the game, you can post intermittent product designs to your extranet so clients, sponsors, and others can review the product as it evolves.

Billing database Use your extranet to give clients real-time information on their bills. They can read and review each invoice you've sent and see the status of payments that have posted to their account.

Once again, if you don't have the staff or technical talent to build your own extranet, you can rent one. Intranets.com, mentioned before, is truly an extranet service; it simply bills itself as an intranet, since most people don't know the difference, and "intranet" is a more popular term than "extranet." But in truth, you can use a site by Intranets.com to collaborate with people outside your team just as easily as you can to communicate with people on your team. And there are other vendors to choose from, as well:

- Adenin (www.adenin.com)

- Intranet Dashboard (www.intranetdashboard.com)

- MindBridge (www.mindbridge.com)

- Vialect (www.vialect.com)

And many more. All these firms have some form of intranet or extranet software for the small to midsized enterprise.

Whether you build your extranet from scratch, lease it from a vendor, or buy software to help you design it, there's one thing you should keep in mind, a problem that many, if not most of us, tend to forget. The truth is, it's easy to build an extranet: The technology is simple and it's long been mastered by most web designers. No fancy coding is needed; no bleeding-edge tricks are required. The hard part is the human part, namely, teaching clients, sponsors, and others to work in a new way, to rely on remote technology to solve problems they'd normally solve by calling the PM. If you design it right, your extranet can easily halve the time you spend talking to people outside your team, but first you have to convince them to use the site often, to trust its content, and to turn to it before they pick up the phone. And that can only be done with time and patience.

Buy the Least Powerful Software

Yes, we said *least* powerful. And we'll explain.

There's a golden rule for buying computers: When in doubt, buy the best you can afford. In other words, if you're not sure if you should buy a machine with a 30GB hard drive or one with a 50GB drive, and you have the money for either, buy the better machine. You'll grow into it, and if not, your software will. (Software gets bigger and bigger each year, as designers add more and more features that add more and more code that takes up more and more space on your drives.) So if you've got the bucks, buy the most machine you can afford. In time you'll need it.

But software is different. Let's take Microsoft Word: It's the *de facto* program for writing memos, letters, reports, forms, and so on. And it can handle them with ease. But it can also interpolate real-time web data, support XML, use IRM (Information Rights Management), and integrate a background MIDI sequence. Not sure what that means? That's the whole point: Word, which is a program we all use by default, has more features than any of us will ever need, much less master. It's one hell of a program, and the truth is, it's too much of a program for most of us to ever use fully.

It's also cheap and ubiquitous (most of us get it by default, something a vendor slapped on our machines), so the glut of features is no big deal. It's simply there and comes with the package. But as a PM, you may have to buy software that's not so cheap, nor so common: project management software, engineering software, financial software, *customer relationship management (CRM)*, and *enterprise resource planning (ERP)*apps, and more. And *those* can run you thousands, tens of thousands, or even hundreds of thousands of dollars.

Why so pricey? In part, because software like that is sold to smaller user groups, so it has to cost more. But these programs are also rich with snazzy features that sound great on paper, advanced options that most of us, in truth, will never use. Like Word, they pack more power than even a power user can master. Yet still we break the bank to afford them, when less costly, simpler versions would do us fine.

(And consider this: Software vendors ensure their future earnings by forcing product upgrades on users. Sometimes there's a good reason for an upgrade—for instance, Netscape went through many upgrades when the Internet was new, evolving to catch up with the medium it was chasing. But most often, upgrades do little but add highly advanced features we don't really need. This rings especially true for upgrades to programs that have been around for years.)

Look at it this way: Would you buy a car that can do 200 miles per hour, when all you need is something to tool around town in? You would if you had money to burn or a dearth of brains. PMs have neither, but for some reason, most of them—most managers in general—overbuy software with features they'll never use or never even need.

If you'd like a rundown of good software for PMs, check out the Software Roundup in the Appendix.

What's in a Name? Learning Document Naming Conventions

Here's a bit of (ugly) reality. These are real documents we've found on a client's corporate network:

ltrrmSep1903.doc (Translation: Letter to Ronnie Michel on September 19, 2003.)

letterRMichel.doc (Translation: Letter to Ronnie Michel on October 22, 2003. We know the date of the letter because we opened the file and read it; clearly, there's no date mentioned in the document's name.)

CTRCT-MICHR-OCTOBER-1-WEAV.doc (Translation: Contract for Ronnie Michel on October 1, 2003, written by Marcus Weaver.)

ronnie's first expense report.xls (Translation: Ronnie Michel's first expense report on October 6, 2003. Once again, we know the report's date since we opened the file and found it; there's no date mentioned in the document's name.)

rmresv2.pdf (Translation: Ronnie Michel's resume, version 2, date unknown.)

MICHELBILL(OCT).doc (Translation: Ronnie Michel's October invoice, 2003.)

Now, if you're the fool who wrote ltrrmSep1903.doc, you might—*might*—remember that it's a letter to Ronnie Michel on September 19, 2003 (and not September of 1903). But let's be honest. Two months after you've written the letter and a year after you're done using Ronnie Michel as a vendor, you won't remember what ltrmSep1903.doc means unless you open the file and read it. And more importantly, a colleague who desperately needs to find the letter won't know what it's named to search for it, and won't even know that it's the right file if he should run across it in some forgotten corner of your hard drive.

To make things worse, all the files above were stored in different places on the corporate network. They weren't collected in a folder named Ronnie

Michel or something just as clear; they were stored in folders based on the documents' authors. So ltrrmSep1903.doc was stored in a folder called MJAKES; letterRMichel.doc was stored in a folder called alansaradon; and that beauty named CTRCT-MICHR-OCTOBER-1-WEAV.doc was stored in a folder named, simply, LEGAL.

Piece of cake, right?

In fact, naming your files like this is fine unless you ever need to

- Store anything

- Find anything

- Read anything

But, on the off chance that you will, we urge you to adopt a standard naming scheme for all your documents. Watch as the files above get renamed using a standard convention:

Letter to Ronnie Michel (09-19-03).doc

Letter to Ronnie Michel (10-22-03).doc

Contract for Ronnie Michel (10-01-03).doc

Expense Report from Ronnie Michel (10-06-03).xls

Resume from Ronnie Michel (version 2).pdf

Invoice from Ronnie Michel (10-31-03).doc

Or, if you'd prefer something more compact, try these filenames:

letter.rmichel.09-19-03.doc

letter.rmichel.10-22-03.doc

contract.rmichel.10-01-03.doc

expense_report.rmichel.10-06-03.xls

resume.rmichel.v2.pdf

invoice.rmichel.10-31-03.doc

What's more, you can store these files in a single folder named—you guessed it—Ronnie Michel (or following the second naming convention above, rmichel). That way your team can easily find anything that pertains to Ronnie, no matter who wrote it. And they'll immediately know what the document is and when it was written based on nothing but its name.

The exact nature of the naming scheme you choose is unimportant, so long as it's clear, common, and used by everyone on your team. We suggest the following, but you can invent one of your own that suits you better:

document_type.description1.description2.version.date.extension

In other words, start with the document type (letter, contract, fax, memo, and so on), followed by a description, followed by a second description if you need it, followed by the version (again, if you need it), followed by the date, followed by the document's extension (.doc, .xls, .pdf, and so forth), and separate (or *delimit*) the sections with a dot ("."). Use lowercase for all letters.

Let's try a few for practice.

A memo to Marty Bevins from Steve Moore on March 4, 2004 becomes

memo.mbevins.smoore.03-04-04.doc

A photo of the new office space you took on May 9, 2004 becomes

photo.office_space.05-09-04.jpg

Version four of the corporate logo they sent to you last week becomes

logo.allied_signal.v4.09-03-04.eps

A document that explains your new naming conventions to your project team becomes

directions.naming_conventions.09-10-04.doc

And so on. Remember to use an underscore ("_") to separate words in the same section, as in allied_signal and naming_conventions above, and separate the elements of a date with dashes. Always mention the year, not merely the month and day. Write all names with the first letter of the first name followed by the full last name. And don't use any punctuation beyond what's mentioned above (the dot, the underscore).

Again, you can use any naming convention you like, so long as it's clear, simple, and approved by your team. We like the one above because it groups like files in alphabetical order in Windows, as follows:

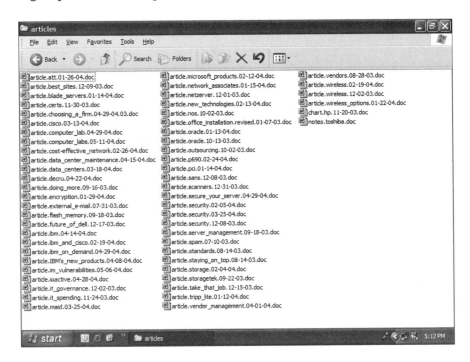

Note how all the articles in this folder are listed in alphabetical order by subject. Anyone, even a new team member, can sort them easily and tell their subject and the date without having to open the file. What's more, if you know you need an article on scanners, you can search for "article.scanners*" and let Windows find it for you.

A Tale of Two Slides

Kay M., a personnel director by trade and a deep-sea diver by passion, had a problem. In two minutes she was supposed to present a list of eight new VPs to the board of directors of Axtron, Inc. (Axtron, whose name we've changed for privacy, made RAM and microchips and was based on the West Coast with a plant in China. All told, they had close to 1,000 employees.)

On Friday, Kay had made a PowerPoint slide with the name and title of each of the VPs. Then she left early to go diving, the last chance she would have before it got too cold for the season. On Monday, she got to the office a few minutes before the meeting and started a search for the PowerPoint slide, which she found within seconds: It was named VPSLIDE.PPT (or so she thought). She put it on disk and walked briskly to the board room.

Once there, she greeted each of the directors by name and asked the eight VPs to stand and be introduced. She popped her disk into a laptop, turned on a projector, and flashed the slide on screen, at which point she promptly had an embolism.

Rather than grab the slide with the list of eight VPs and their titles, she'd grabbed a slide with the list of eight VPs and their *salaries*. The two slides were nearly the same in name: VPSLIDE.PPT and VEEP-SLIDE.PPT. She'd merely confused one for the other.

Kay's boss, Melanie, had been after her for more than a month to use a standard naming convention for all their files, but Kay had put it off more than once. The result? When two of the new VPs left over salary disputes after the board meeting, Axtron decided that Kay should follow them out the door. ✐

Gadgets You Need (Part 1)

There's no way around it: We live in an ultra-wired world. These days you can't leave the office without taking the office with you, in the form of cell phones, pagers, beepers, Palms, notebooks and more. And while you can easily shed a few of these gadgets and lead a perfectly happy life, today's PM is bound to be in touch with her team at all times. That means you'll always have a device or two with you. But the upside—and yes, there is an upside—is this: Some of these tools do more than chain you to your desk. They make your work simpler. And they make your load lighter.

Take your Palm Pilot. Today's Palms are light years ahead of the clunkers we bought only two years ago. They're thin, light, and boast wireless connections as well. Some even have cell phones built in, such as the Treo smartphone (http://web.palmone.com). This little wonder has all the old features of Palms: a calendar, task list, contacts, notes, and so forth, plus some new ones like wireless e-mail, web browsing, and IM (instant messaging), as well as a nifty digital camera for quick shots of team members, construction sites, or anything else you need to document. Its built-in keyboard makes text entry a breeze, and the on-board phone has a speakerphone and integrated call logs to boot.

But the true power of the Treo—as well as any Palm or Windows mobile device (these are made by HP, Dell, and others and use a small version of the Windows operating system)—is the software you can add to it. Skeptical? Point your web browser to Handango at www.handango.com and browse the software titles. You'll find everything from time sheets to expense tracking and a database of postal codes, not to mention city guides for Asia, Europe, the U.S., and South America, language translators, GPS systems, spreadsheets, financial calculators, inventory systems, barometers, sales logs, thousands of e-books (including some on project management), image viewers, outliners, mind maps, and dozens and dozens of *PIMs* (or personal information managers). Curious? Take a look at the Agendus PIM by Iambic Software (www.iambic.com). It not only keeps your calendar, tasks, and contacts in good order, it lets you link all three together to build a complete contact history for everyone you know. You can even view maps, photos, and birthday reminders.

Beyond the gee-whiz gadgetry of these mini software marvels are the hardcore project-tracking programs that any PM using a Palm or Pocket PC should never be without. Take ProjectHand 2 by Natara Software (www.natara.com). It's an advanced task manager with integrated Gantt charts, resource lists, cost tracking, and many of the features you'd find in Microsoft Project. (In fact, it even integrates with Project, so you can discreetly tweak your project plans on an airplane or while sitting in a boring meeting.) For PMs who organize large meetings and other events, EventPlan by Watters-Edge (www.watters-edge.com) lets you store guest lists with contact info, track vendors and their bills, build event timelines, write budgets, and more. And these are merely two of dozens of programs you can buy for under $50.

Gadgets You Need (Part 2)

Of course, palmtops like the Treo or the HP iPAQ (www.hp.com) are just one type of gadget that can make your life simpler (and help you work better, to boot).

Believe it or not, even an MP3 player can have a business use. All too often the busy PM has no time to read, be it a business book or simply *The New York Times*. Books on tape are good, but they're only useful in cars, and while most of us have a lengthy commute to the office, it would be nice to hear David Allen's *Getting Things Done: The Art of Stress-Free Productivity* (Penguin Books, 2003) or Roger Fisher's *Getting To Yes: Negotiating Agreement Without Giving In* (Penguin Books, 1991) whenever you please. Enter Audible at www.audible.com. Audible is a website that lets you download books, radio programs, magazines, and daily papers to your MP3 player, Palm, or Pocket PC. And their selection is huge, with everything from language programs (useful for PMs who work overseas, or work with overseas teams) to *The Wall Street Journal* to *The Harvard Business Review*, all in audible format.

And while you're toying around with some of the titles at Audible, don't forget the rarely used but highly useful functions of your cell phone. Ever smaller and smaller, today's phones can surf the Web, send and receive e-mail, download news, and even integrate with project intranets and extranets. (For instance, the products at Intranets.com let you access your contact lists and member directories right from your web-enabled cell phone.)

Of course, the trick in using these gadgets is learning to master them, not letting them master you. If you're not careful, you can easily bog yourself down in the intricacies of every gadget you own and become such an egghead that you rarely communicate the old fashioned way: that is, by meeting people in person and having a nice, long chat. (Remember the days before e-mail?) Bear in mind that gadgets should make your life simpler, and if you buy an expensive toy and find that you just can't use it, no matter how you try, drop it. Too many people—most of them smart, savvy people like you—hold on to technology that does nothing for them simply because they've spent too much on it. Don't be one of them. Let your gadgets enhance your life, not destroy it.

Dealing with Luddites

Let's take a trip to the dictionary, shall we?

Luddites are people who oppose technological change. The name comes from a group of British workers, masked, anonymous, and violent, who burned down textile factories in 1816, in the (mistaken) belief that new, labor-saving machines would put them out of work.

Today, the word "Luddite" refers to people who insist on having their secretaries print their e-mail and read it aloud. (Sound familiar?) Luddites still own a Betamax. They use Polaroids. Their kitchen blender is about as technical as they get. Most have a computer at work—because, to be frank, they have to—but they regard it with suspicion, touching it gently if at all, the way you touch a rabid gerbil.

Luddites do not use intranets.

Luddites do not use extranets.

Luddites use cell phones as doorstops.

Luddites can be a danger to your team. Today, the discipline of project management is inherently technical. True, it began in the 1950s and was mostly done with paper and pen, but it's evolved, and rare is the project team that doesn't e-mail, Google, and meet in cyberspace.

Luddites slow all this down. When you send a meeting reminder by e-mail, they miss the meeting, not having read their mail. (Or, just as likely, they've tried to read it but mistakenly deleted it before they were able to open it.) When you post a revised statement of scope to the intranet, they ask for a hard copy (which in turn makes you print one out and hand it over, wasting time and money alike). If you tell them to write a status report and save it to the network so you can retrieve it and read it, they save it to their hard drive (or better, to a floppy) with a name like THISISMYSTATUS-REPORT.doc. (You doubt it? That was a true example.)

Unavoidably, you'll run across a Luddite or two in your career, and if you've offended the gods, you'll have one posted to your team. The question, of course, is how you deal with him, and how you forcibly evolve this loveable, curmudgeonly Neanderthal into *homo technologicus*. To that end we offer a few points.

Take it slow. Remember that all technology has a learning curve (unless of course you're 12, in which case everything from your Pocket PC to your DVD is totally simple, dude). And the learning curve for Luddites is abnormally slow. Here, patience is not merely a virtue; it's a requisite, and you'll never get a Luddite to use WebEx if you can't show him how to do it gently.

Invest in training. Just because a Luddite is slow to attach files to e-mail does not mean he's stupid. In fact, most Luddites are bright, seasoned workers who've been around the block a time or two. Their deficits aside, they can be a boon to your project team. So take the time and money to get them some training. If your Luddite is truly a gem *without* knowing how to read your intranet, imagine how good he'll be once he does.

Insist on good design. Remember that your intranet, extranet, and database apps are all within your power to design. Whether you rent them, buy them, or build them from scratch, you'll always have some control over their layout. And all too often they're clunky, confusing, and poorly imagined. Yes, it costs more to hire the best designers, but do whatever you can to get top talent that knows how to build or customize software so it's implicitly user-friendly. Not only will your Luddites be thankful (and quicker to learn the technology), but you will be, too.

Use some common sense. Just because a technology exists does *not* mean you should use it. Don't be too quick to buy the latest and greatest software, the newest gadgets, or other toys on the bleeding edge. Why? They may promise the world, but they rarely deliver. New technology is often untested. It has quirks and bugs. And when you buy it for your project team, you not only force them to learn it (often an imposition) but you open your project up to risk—here, the risk of faulty tools. Luddites who've taken the time—slowly and painfully, to be sure—to learn a piece of software often resent a new upgrade that demands their attention again. The bottom line? Invest in technology wisely. Buy it when you need it, and never simply because you can.

Dealing with Eggheads

By and large, eggheads are nerds, but there's a species of egghead we'd like to address in particular: the (dreaded) computer geek.

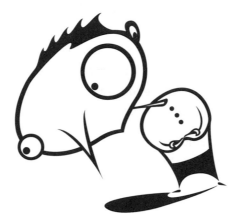

These eggheads are not your enemy, though you might think they are. They're not the bane of your life, though at times it could seem that way. You should not, no matter how much you want to, pelt them with rotten eggs, stink-bomb their cars, or beat them about the head with a curling iron. Not that it's wrong to do so. God knows at times they deserve it. It's just that you might get caught.

We're kidding. In truth, eggheads—and computer geeks in particular—get a bum rap. They have very tough jobs. They have to make the network run, and as such, they deal with equipment failure, bad software, and third-rate vendors all day long. It would test the patience of a saint, much less a twenty-something American male who's just trying to make a living. Worse, they're made to deal with morons like us who still look for the Any key (and, most annoyingly, are proud of it).

Here are some true stories in that vein:

- A new art director at an ad agency called the IT group to complain about not having access to the network. "I'm staring at my screen right now," she said, a bit huffily, "and I can't see anything." The tech led her through several steps to fix the problem, and when none of them worked, he was forced to leave his desk (and abandon his current task thus interrupting his day) to make an office call. When he got there, he quickly found the problem: The monitor was turned off.

- The VP of sales at a large chain of bookstores called the CIO at home (on a Sunday, no less) to ask if the network was down. "I can't log in," she said—and to her credit was polite about it. "It won't take my password." The problem? After 10 minutes on the phone, the CIO—whose job is *not* to run tech support—realized that the veep's CAPS LOCK key was on.

- The head of a small airline liked to use his CD-ROM drive as a cup holder. In one year he spilled coffee or Coke into his machine four different times.

- "I can't get to our website," said a junior sales rep on a tech support call. "I think it's down. And frankly I'm getting sick of it. Can't you keep it working?" Of course, he failed to see he was typing the site's domain name wrong, and the domain name was simply the name of the firm he worked for.

Most of the time, we don't see how badly we treat our friends the computer geeks. Our systems go down, and we spend a few minutes trying to make them work again. When that fails, we call tech support in angry, corrosive moods, and without knowing it, we often confuse the hellish machines for the people who fix them, taking our problems out on the poor geek who did nothing wrong but answer the phone.

In return he often snaps backs, acting as though you're dumb enough to eat nails. It's a vicious cycle, and it's part of the reason that eggheads quit their jobs so often: They're tired of the abuse.

PMs should know better—and do better. These days, project management is all about the cutting edge. Gone are the days when budgets were done by hand and tasks were tacked up on bulletin boards. Now they're published to project intranets and pushed out to team members' PDAs. Teams as far apart as Chicago and Sri Lanka work together in web meetings, and clients and sponsors get their updates on slick, high-end extranets.

Of course, you can't do this without the help of eggheads, so as a PM, you should make it your job to form a pact with your company's techies. Get to know them and learn to respect their talents. (If you do, you'll find they'll learn to respect yours.) Make sure your team treats them well. And time permitting, go so far as to buy them lunch or bring them some donuts every so often. Why? Because they're human, and like everyone else on earth, they remember a kindness done. They'll give your projects top priority; they'll give you quicker—and better—support; and when you're in trouble and need a hand, they'll whip up a database or put up a website just for you.

In the end, it can mean the difference between your project's success and failure.

Avoiding Infosclerosis

From The American Heritage Dictionary (Delta, 2001):

scle·ro·sis

noun

plural scle·ro·ses

a. A thickening or hardening of a body part, as of an artery, especially from excessive formation of fibrous tissue. b. A disease characterized by this thickening or hardening.

Sclerosis: It's a disease. It happens to veins and arteries when too much gunk clogs them up and makes them hard. And it can happen with technology as well, when too much information—too much raw data to read and remember—starts to clog your life.

Answer this question: How much e-mail is in your inbox? Ten pieces? A hundred? A thousand? Is it neatly filed and stored in folders, or merely clumped together as it came in?

What's your desk look like? Is it littered with papers, memos, books, and reports? Do you have letters to read, mail to open, forms to sign? Can you see your desk pad?

Open your My Documents folder from your Desktop. Type Ctrl+A to select all its items, right-click your mouse on one of the folders or files, and choose Properties. How many files do you have? (You'll see the answer in the top part of the Properties dialog box that appears.) More than a hundred? More than five hundred? Can you locate any one of them in five seconds flat? Do you even know what they are, much less *where* they are?

How many magazines do you get, at home or at work? How many of them are more than a month old, sitting unread in a heap on your floor?

It's said the average copy of *The New York Times* has more information than a medieval peasant was apt to receive in his entire life, and the online version at www.nytimes.com not only has today's issue, but issues that date back to the 1940s. What's more, that's only one of 9403 online papers listed at Yahoo! at the time this book was written. Who knows what the next 10 years will bring?

Get the picture? We're inundated, saturated, and submerged in data. We're drowing. We're heading towards the bottom of the ocean. No matter how fast you read, there's no way to process, much less remember, all the info you get in a day. Schedules. Memos. Voicemails. Over time it all becomes a blur, and you harden to its presence. You stop using it. It begins to sink you.

But it doesn't have to. Believe it or not, there are ways to cope with the glut of information that clogs our networks and clouds our brains:

Deal with e-mail immediately. All too often we open a piece of e-mail when it arrives, read it, and leave it there to act on later. Big mistake. Over time your inbox becomes an endless list of e-mails, some of them useful, most of them useless, and all of them waiting to be filed. Instead, check your e-mail two or three times a day, and read, reply, and store what you need to immediately. If cleanliness is next to godliness, a clean inbox—an utter rarity but a blessing—is sure to please the Almighty. Better yet, it's sure to please you.

Use filters. First and foremost, use a spam filter. Outlook 2003, perhaps the world's most useful e-mail tool, has one built in. You can buy others from Norton, McAfee, and more. Nearly six billion spam e-mails were caught and deleted by e-mail tracker Postini in September of 2004, and that's only the work of one firm. So why waste your time reading and deleting trash?

Use a document naming scheme. We've explained this one above. While it may take some time to get used to, it will, in the end, let you sort and retrieve your documents at a moment's notice, with a master's accuracy.

Use the network, dammit. Far too often team members share files by sending them back and forth by e-mail. This not only makes for more e-mail (which you'll leave in your inbox until it begins to grow mold), it wastes space on corporate networks. When you send a file as an attachment by e-mail, you create at least two copies of the file: one in your Sent Items folder, the other in your colleague's inbox. That's a useless duplication. Instead, post the document to the network— where you'll store only one copy of it—and send your colleague a link.

Then he can download it, read it, revise it, and put it back in its network place. You won't have endless copies of documents (and endless versions you can't track) floating through your wires.

Throw it out. You'd be amazed to see what people hold on to. Most of us have paper on our desks that has been there for more than a month—and sometimes, more than several. If it's been there for more than a week, get rid of it. Dump it. Trash it. Avail yourself of the circular file. Chances are you don't really need it. And if you think you do, file it—now.

Get smart with software. Believe it or not, there's software designed to help you cope with information overload. One such product is Enfish Find (www.enfish.com), which, once installed on your PC, begins to read, index, and cross-reference every single document, e-mail, attachment, website, presentation, database, spreadsheet, and graphic you use. To find something, you simply type a keyword into Enfish (say, the name of your client) and it spits out a list of all the documents that have that name in its title or text, no matter where the file's located.

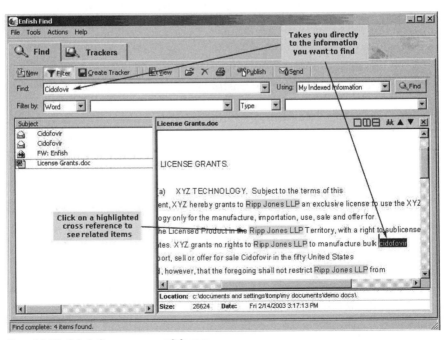

Copyright Enfish Software, www.enfish.com.

Try web portals. If you're always using the Web to search for info or read the news, try a web portal. Sites like news.yahoo.com and www.google.com/news cull the best articles from thousands of papers and present them all in one place, sorted by topic.

Tame those photos. How many photos and graphics do you store on your PC? Maybe none. Maybe thousands. If you're in the latter group, it's likely your photos are randomly stored across your hard drive with names like DSC00083.jpg (which is how they're named by the digital cameras that take them). Of course there's no way to know that DSC00083.jpg is a picture of Aunt Franny eating flapjacks, or more likely, the new construction site you've been working on. A program like Picasa (www.picasa.com, brought to you by Google) lets you store and sort your photos in one place, as well as search them by keyword and category. You can also build slideshows and upload your photos to websites to share with your team.

Blazing Shortcuts in Microsoft Project

For most PMs, Microsoft Project (www.microsoft.com/project) is both their salvation and the bane of their lives. Love it or hate it (and yes, we love it), you have to admit that it's one hell of a program—in fact, in the last few years it's made some impressive strides. Now more than ever, it's poised to fight Primavera (www.primavera.com) and other pricey, fancy, high-end software for the World Cup of project management programs.

But, as for its design, it's a just a mite bulky. Unless you've got an abnormally large screen (the kind that most companies aren't willing to spring for), the interface is a bit crowded. You can't always see what you need to without scrolling, and you have to hunt down important commands with your mouse when they're not at the tips of your fingers.

That is, until now...If you're pressed for time and yoked to Microsoft Project, as most of us are, you need to get the most from your keyboard and its many shortcuts. They'll let you get more out of Project, and use it more efficiently, too. Of course, finding a list of shortcuts is roughly as easy as finding the socks you lost in the dryer, so we've assembled one for you. The bulk of these shortcuts work in all versions of Project, but some work only in Project 2003:

Activity	Shortcut
New document	Ctrl+N
Open document	Ctrl+O
Save document	Ctrl+S
Print document	Ctrl+P
Spell check	F7
Cut cell	Ctrl+X
Copy cell	Ctrl+C
Paste cell	Ctrl+V

Activity	Shortcut
Insert hyperlink	Ctrl+K
Link tasks	Ctrl+F2
Unlink tasks	Ctrl+Shift+F2
Task information	Shift+F2
Assign resources	Alt+F10
Zoom in	Ctrl+/
Zoom out	Ctrl+*
Go to selected task	Ctrl+Shift+F5
Open help	F1
Outdent	Alt+Shift+Left arrow
Indent	Alt+Shift+Right arrow
Show subtasks	Alt+Shift+Plus (+)
Hide subtasks	Alt+Shift+Minus (–)
Find	Ctrl+F
Replace	Ctrl+H
Go to	Ctrl+G
Fill down	Ctrl+D
Fill right	Ctrl+R
New task	Insert

The Myth of Multitasking

If, by chance, you're like the rest of us—and you know you are—you try to do a bevy of tasks all at once, including the following:

- Talk on the phone

- Read e-mail

- Listen to voicemail

- Sip coffee

- Write yourself notes

- Write memos

- Write letters

- Read project updates

- Put on makeup or shave

- Drive

Well, let's hope you're not driving while doing all that other stuff, though, to be frank, we've known people who have. The point is that multi-tasking—otherwise known as doing 10 things at once—has become a glorified skill. It's now the end-all and be-all of corporate efficiency for both the average worker and the PM in particular, whose job, it seems, is to juggle a dozen balls at a time without dropping one. That's seen as a sign of talent these days—and indeed, there's a certain skill in being able to keep the plates spinning. In fact, if you go on a job interview, you're likely to be asked if you multitask. (And only the fool answers no.)

So we'll let you in on a secret. Multitasking is a sham. It's a joke, a waste, and a piece of litter on the highway of high efficiency. Apart from Enron's so-called stable bottom line, it's the biggest lie that's been foisted on American workers in the last decade, and maybe two.

Why? In 2001, a group of folks at the University of Michigan (all of whom have Ph.D.s after their names) studied the myth of multitasking, and found out that 20 to 40 percent of our productivity is used up in *task-switching*, that is, the time it takes you to move from one task to another and start to focus on the new task.

Here's the bottom line: If you do 10 things at once, you switch between all 10 things *at least* once; thus if it takes you three seconds to switch between tasks, you've lost 30 seconds on nothing but task-switching. Of course, most of us take more than three seconds to switch between tasks. What's more, there's also the time it takes to re-orient yourself to the task at hand, which can take a second or two on up to a minute for complex tasks. That's time out the window, too, never to be seen again.

If, instead, you simply do one task at once, and move from task to task in a linear, not matrixed, fashion, you'll find that you get more done in less time. And you'll find that you improve not only the quantity of your work, but its quality, too.

Of course, it's hard for a PM to justify the seemingly leisurely pace of doing one thing at a time, and not 10. Your team may question you. Your boss may question you. In fact, they may demand that you juggle their needs, requests, demands, questions, petitions, assertions, clamors, and cries all while handling the phone, sending e-mail, writing a memo, and putting out fires. But remember the piece of political advice we gave you in Chapter 4, "Surviving the Corporate Jungle": Be assertive. Time, in spite of being a universal and the one thing that evades us all, is also the one thing we can truly *own*. We can use it right; we can make it ours. And in doing that we can assert a simple ethic of management, namely, that time is precious and work—our work, which takes us out of home and away from our families and apart from the things we love—is a thing of value. And no thing of value was ever rushed. True, you'll have to multitask as part of your job. You work in a complex environment called an office where you're pulled from one side to the other in dozens of ways at once. But it's your choice to assert your rights and manage your time as well—and as efficiently—as possible. After all, a good PM knows how to get things done; a *great* PM knows how to do great things. And you can't approach excellence if you can't manage the one thing we all have in common: too little time.

So, the next time you sit down at your desk and flip on your screen, close all your open programs. That's right. Close every single one. Don't, as we're all apt to do, keep your e-mail running in the background, so you can read new e-mail as soon as you get it. Don't keep two copies of Microsoft Word and one copy of Excel up and running, along with your web browser and Microsoft Project. Simply focus on the task at hand, using only the software you need. Move from that task to the next and make a conscious effort not to juggle. If your colleagues demand your attention—and hence, demand that you do two things at once—assertively (but politely) show them the door.

The result? You'll blaze through your work and leave the office early, the better to get home and cook, clean, call your friends, help the kids with their homework, do the laundry, watch TV, read the paper, take out the trash, surf the Web, answer your e-mail, get to the bank, go to the store, walk the dog, feed the cat, and more. Just don't do it all at once, of course.

Appendix

The Chicken Herder's Toolkit

Our goal is to make you an expert chicken herder, the kind of PM who can whip a team into shape and get projects done in record time. Since the right tools always help, we've assembled a few of them for you in this appendix.

Useful Templates and Tools

We're a little full of ourselves, so we think we've given you some good—even great—advice in the last six chapters. But even the best advice is useless if you can't act on it, so here's a quick guide to the forms you can use to put into practice the Herding Chickens methods in your organization.

You can download all of these forms from www.herdingchickens.com. They're yours to use free of charge.

Action Items template

After a meeting you'll often have a set of tasks you need to assign to your team. Use this form to do just that, noting the task, due date, status, and other data.

Herding Chickens

ACTION ITEMS LOG • • • • • • •

Use this template to build a log of your project's action items.

#	Action Item	Priority	Date Created	Assigned To	Due Date	Status	Notes

RFC template

There are times when you'll need to get the input of your project sponsor or executive. When you do, you'll want a written record of what he said, in case you ever need to justify a decision you made to keep the project on time and on budget. This form can be used to get a sponsor's instructions on any point of clarification (hence the title, *RFC*, or *Request for Clarification*) in your project.

REQUEST FOR CLARIFICATION • • • •

There are times when you'll need input from your project sponsor or another executive. Use this form to keep a written record of his/her comments and instructions.

PROJECT	DATE SUBMITTED
SUBMITTED BY	DATE RECEIVED

ISSUE

PROJECT IMPACT

SPONSOR'S COMMENTS/INSTRUCTIONS

PM'S NOTES

Communications Plan template

As a PM, you've got tons of work to do, not the least of which is keeping in touch with vital members of your project group—the sponsor, the client, key executives, vendors, and of course, the project team itself. Sometimes the task of keeping everyone informed can be so complex that it needs a plan. The communications plan template will help you organize your project communication to a level of systematic precision. (Please note: Due to technical considerations, only a part of the Communications Plan template is reproduced on the next page. The real thing is several pages long. You can find it, in its entirety, on the Herding Chickens website or the Sybex website. Your choice.)

Herding Chickens

COMMUNICATIONS PLAN ● ● ● ● ● ● ● ●

Use this template to build or enhance your project communications plan.

DATE	PREPARED BY
PROJECT	REVISION

Objectives

Good communication is crucial to the success of this project. With that in mind, this plan is meant to help us with the following:

- Enter the first objective here
- Enter the second objective here
- Enter the third objective here

Target Audience (Internal)

Your target audience includes people you plan to communicate with in a frequent and systematic way such as your project sponsor, executive team, clients, and so forth.

First Target Audience (Internal)
How often will you communicate with him/them?
☐ Daily   ☐ Weekly   ☐ Monthly   ☐ Quarterly   ☐ Other: _____
How will you do so?
☐ Phone   ☐ Fax   ☐ E-mail   ☐ Extranet   ☐ Meeting   ☐ WebEx
Who will do this?
Notes/Comments

Pleasure & Displeasure List template

A project's success is relative. You may think it went swimmingly, but unless your sponsor agrees, you're plumb out of luck. The same can be said for any number of key figures in your project—clients, executives, and corporate bigwigs, to name a few. Use the Pleasure and Displeasure List to educate your team on meeting those expectations.

Herding Chickens

PLEASURE & DISPLEASURE LIST • •

Use this template to build your Pleasure and Displeasure List, as explained in Chapter 2.

Person/Group	Pleasure	Displeasure

Post Mortem template

When a project's over, you should dissect it with your team to see what can be improved the next time around. It's called the post mortem, and this form will guide you through it.

Herding Chickens

PROJECT POST MORTEM • • • • • • • •

Use this template to conduct your project's post mortem meeting. A post mortem is a team session where you review what worked and did not work with a recently completed project. You should also interview all project stakeholders, such as the sponsor or client, to get your results.

DATE	PREPARED BY
PROJECT	REVISION

POST MORTEM MEETING DATE	MEETING PLACE

Man-Hours/Effort Estimates

- At the start of your project (during the planning phase), how much time or man-hours did you estimate for this project?

- How much time or man-hours did you spend on this project?

Budget/Cost

- How much did you plan to spend on this project?

- How much did you spend in reality?

Staff

- Were you correct in your initial staffing estimates? If not, why? What changed?

Range Estimate template

Estimates are often wrong. You can make them more precise with a range estimate, one that includes a range of costs for each item in your project budget. This form will help you write a detailed range estimate.

Herding Chickens

RANGE ESTIMATE • • • • • • •

Use this template to build your project's own range estimate. Just type over the entries below and add or remove columns as you need to.

CONFIDENTIAL

DATE		PREPARED BY	
PROJECT		REVISION	

Item	Low Cost	High Cost	Total Low Cost	Total High Cost
Item 1	$900,000	$1,100,000	$900,000	$1,100,000
Item 2	$500,000	$700,000	$1,400,000	$1,800,000

Responsibilities Matrix template

In a large project it's hard to keep tabs on who does what. In fact, if you've got a project team with 10, 20, or 30 people, you may need a formal way to list all their duties—not only for reference, but for your sanity, as well. Enter the responsibilities matrix, which helps you nail down your team members' functions.

RESPONSIBILITIES MATRIX • • • • • •

Use this template to build your project's own responsibilities matrix. Just type over the entries below and add or remove columns as you need to.

Activity	Sponsor	PM	Steering Committee	Finance	Legal
(To add columns to this table, click Table ➤ Insert ➤ Columns to the Left.)					
Project Charter	I	C	A		
Comm. Plan	A	C		I	I
Meeting Schedule	A	C			
Job Cost Reports	R	I		C	
Contracts		I		I	C
Scope Changes	R	C		I	I
(To add rows to this table, click Table ➤ Insert ➤ Rows Above or Table ➤ Insert ➤ Rows Below.)					

KEY

- **A**   Approves the deliverable.
- **R**   Reviews the deliverable.
- **C**   Creates the deliverable.
- **I**   Gives input on the deliverable.
- **N**   Is notified when a deliverable is complete.
- **M**   Manages the deliverable.

Skills Matrix template

This form can be used to keep a running list of your team member's talents, including their special skills.

Herding Chickens

SKILLS MATRIX ● ● ● ● ● ● ● ●

Use this template to build your team's skills matrix. Just type over the entries below and add or remove columns as you need to.

Skill	Team Member 1	Team Member 2	Team Member 3	Team Member 4	Team Member 5	Team Member 6
(To add columns to this table, click Table ➢ Insert ➢ Columns to the Left.)						
Skill 1	F/S/E	F/S/E	F/S/E	F/S/E	F/S/E	F/S/E
Skill 2						
Skill 3						
Skill 4						
Skill 5						
Skill 6						
(To add rows to this table, click Table ➢ Insert ➢ Rows Above or Table ➢ Insert ➢ Rows Below.)						

KEY

- **F**   means the team member is *f*amiliar with that program or skill set.
- **S**   means he or she is *s*killed at that function.
- **E**   stands for *e*xpert.

Status Report template

Along with your action items, the status report is one of the key documents in the daily use of project management.

Herding Chickens

WEEKLY STATUS REPORT ● ● ● ● ● ●

Use this template to build your weekly status report. Simply type over the entries below.

Things we've accomplished this week:

Entry 1
Entry 2
Entry 3

Things to accomplish next week:

Entry 1
Entry 2
Entry 3

Special resource requirements:

Entry 1
Entry 2
Entry 3

Immediate problems to be addressed:

Entry 1
Entry 2
Entry 3

Stoplight Chart template

Most often, project sponsors like it short and sweet. The stoplight chart is a way to communicate the status of your project in a quick and simple format. It takes only minutes to write and takes your sponsors even less time to read.

Herding Chickens

STOPLIGHT CHART • • • • • • • • • • •

Use this template to build your project's own stoplight chart. Simply fill in the tasks below, then copy and paste the colored icons on the right to show the status of each task.

Task/Item	Status
Task 1	●
Task 2	●
Task 3	●
Task 4	
Task 5	
Task 6	
Task 7	
Task 8	
Task 9	
Task 10	
Task 11	
Task 12	
Task 13	
Task 14	
Task 15	

These forms can be useful tools to run your project. But the uber-tool, the single most vital tool in your chest, is your project intranet. It can halve your work and double your output in one fell swoop.

Of course, building an intranet is nothing to laugh at. Beyond the technology, the toughest part is knowing what content you want and how to use it. The following mind map lays out the contents of a prospective intranet; use it to talk to your IT group and get the ball rolling.

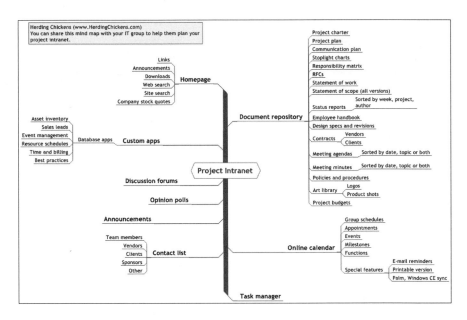

Software Roundup

The right software can make or break your project, so choose it with care. Believe it or not, there's more to the project management software universe than simply Microsoft Project. In fact, the choices are nearly endless, so we've assembled a few of them here to kick-start your search.

The two most popular and probably most useful software products you'll use in project management are Microsoft Project and Primavera.

Microsoft Project www.microsoft.com/project

This is the granddaddy of project software, the one program that everyone needs. Microsoft Project helps you with all the basics—calendars, schedules, assignments, resource planning, and so on—and lets you publish your plans to a project intranet. It also comes with scads of templates to kick-start your work. These include office move plans, new product plans, direct mail plans, and more.

Primavera www.primavera.com

Primavera, though less popular than Microsoft Project and often more expensive, is still a strong choice of project management software. Its many versions include IT, engineering and construction, maintenance and turnaround, new product development, and more.

AceProject www.aceproject.com

This web-based software is a great alternative to Microsoft Project and Primavera for simple projects or small companies. In fact, the Hosted Basic plan is free, though it only supports five projects, five users, and 30 tasks at once. Be sure to visit the website for a live demo.

BPS Project www.bpsproject.com

Another web-based solution, BPS Project offers all the standard features and then some, including planning, budgets, and issue and document management. Since the software is web-based, it's perfect for virtual teams.

Project Insight www.projectinsight.com

Bubbling with features, Project Insight offers Gantt charts, calendars, tasks, to-do lists, issues, risk, resource, time and billing, discussions, auto alerts, e-mail notifications, and project dashboard reports. It also integrates with Microsoft Project and Microsoft Office.

Infowit www.infowit.com

Infowit is the only project management app designed for graphic artists, designers, ad agencies, marketers, and other creative types. Highly modular, it offers estimates, schedules, client review, document tracking, approval tracking, time cards, purchasing, prospecting control, and other features as well.

Project.net www.project.net

Like most of its brethren, Project.net can be used for the complete life of the project, from conception to completion. But this software has a unique design: It has a Personal Workspace, a Project Workspace, and a Business Workspace. The Personal Workspace gives people access to their own work, tasks, and so on; the Project Workspace gives teams access to joint calendars, task lists, announcements, and more; and the Business Workspace gives people in the enterprise (but not on the project team) a way to check in on projects and view their status.

mji teamworks www.mjiteamworks.com

Designed for multi-project management, resource management, issue and incident management, case management, campaign management, and timesheet management, mji teamworks also lets you share your project data with third parties such as clients, vendors, and business partners.

xpdproject www.xpdoffice.com

xpdproject, which has all the basics and then some, such as earned value management (EVM) and advanced security features, is fully web-based, meaning you won't have to install it or run it in-house. And being web-based, it's great for virtual teams.

Copper 2004 www.copperproject.com

Copper is known for its simple but snazzy interface—in fact, it's so easy to learn that you won't have to spend time, talent, and money on training. It comes in standard, pro, and hosted versions for as little as $35 per month.

Glossary

5-15 report

The 5-15 report is written once a week. It should take your CEO or project sponsor five minutes to read and should take you no more than 15 minutes to write. The report should include four sections: first, a section on how you made the company money this week; second, a section on how you saved the company money this week; third, a list of crises you prevented; and fourth, a list of anything you need from the CEO or sponsor.

80/20 rule

See *Pareto's Law*.

action meetings

Action meetings are designed for getting something done and/or making decisions. Action meetings are filled with give and take and highly interactive discussions. They're always followed up by action item reports or meeting minutes. See also *information meetings; standup meetings*.

assumption

Simply put, an assumption is something you assume will happen in the course of your project. For instance, you assume that you'll have enough money to finish the project, that your sponsor will give it his full support, that steel will stay at a constant price for the next year, and so on. Assumptions should be carefully exposed and considered since they often turn out to be false, and it pays to plan for every contingency.

At The Tables

See *ATTs*.

ATTs (At The Tables)

ATTs are a meeting's principals, the men and women who sit at the conference table and not along the wall, as junior staff may. ATTs are expected to talk and contribute to the meeting, as opposed to In the Rooms (ITRs). See also *ITRs; OTPs.*

audit

An audit is a careful, detailed review of your project by people outside your team or even outside your firm. Audits are often made when something's gone wrong, say, to review a project's past financial performance, its adherence to project management procedures, and the like. As such, they depend on the paper trail that your project leaves behind it—your statement of scope, project charter, change requests, memos, e-mails, and more. Be sure to distinguish audits from independent project reviews (IPRs). See also *IPR.*

BCP (business continuity plan)

A BCP is a plan designed to get your business through a disaster such as a fire, flood, or the sudden death of a key executive. Its goal is to help you restore your business to normal as soon as possible. A well-made BCP should be written long before disaster strikes, and it should be tested and planned well in advance in case of a catastrophe occurs. See also *DR.*

body language

Body language refers to nonverbal communication such as hand gestures and eye movements that are made with the body.

business continuity plan (BCP)

See *BCP.*

business impact analysis

A business impact analysis is the process, often complex, of analyzing the impact on your business of several kinds of disasters such as fire, flood, or violent storms.

change management

Change management is the process of controlling corporate change in a way that disrupts business as little as possible. In this context, change management does not refer to controlling change on a single project. Rather, it refers to controlling change across the enterprise, such as when installing a new call center, changing a business process, and so on (each of which, one can note, are individual projects in themselves).

CM (crisis management)

Crisis management (CM) is the way that a firm responds to any kind of disaster, from a fire that destroys its data center to bad publicity or the loss of key executives. CM's goal is to lessen or even avoid the negative effects of disaster.

constraints

A constraint is a restriction on your project. As a project manager, you have to balance one constraint with all others to make the project a success. The four constraints that apply to every project are scope, quality, time, and resources.

contingency planning

See *CP*.

cost-to-complete

The cost-to-complete refers to the amount that a project component (such as steel, salaries, supplies, and so on) will cost until the project is finished. If you need 1000 tons of steel to finish your project and steel sells for a dollar a ton, your cost-to-complete for steel is $1000. See also *cost-to-date*; *job cost report*; *total cost*.

cost-to-date

The cost-to-date refers to the amount that a project component (such as steel, salaries, supplies, and so on) has cost to date. See also *cost-to-complete*; *job cost report*; *total cost*.

CP (contingency planning)

Contingency planning refers to the act of planning for project risks and disruptions. For instance, if your project depends on the use of a supercomputer, you should have a plan if the computer goes down or if your access to it is somehow cut off. Your contingency plan will let you continue your project even in the face of such adversity.

crisis management

See *CM*.

CRM (customer relationship management)

CRM refers to the software and systems that let you interact with your customer base. Often this involves a large database that tracks customers, orders, complaints, and so forth. Popular makers of CRM software include Oracle (www.oracle.com) and Siebel (www.siebel.com).

current state

The current state of a business function refers to its present condition, as opposed to its future state (namely, the way you envision it to work when your project is done).

customer relationship management

See *CRM*.

disaster recovery

See *DR*.

DR (disaster recovery)

The field of disaster recovery includes the plans that let your firm continue to work after a disaster or a disruption to service such as a power outage. A business continuity plan is a key element of disaster recovery. See also *BCP*.

elastic stress point

In engineering, an elastic stress point is the farthest point to which an object will bend yet still bounce back into shape. Any motion beyond the elastic stress point will permanently deform the object. In like manner, changing the parameters of a project too much will cause it to yield unexpected—and sometimes disastrous—results.

enterprise resource planning

See *ERP*.

ERP (enterprise resource planning)

ERP is a type of software that lets users plan inventory, sales, marketing, order tracking, customer service, and finance in one package.

extranet

An extranet is a private website that you, your team, and people outside your team such as sponsors or clients can view with a username and password. Extranets are used to communicate with important people outside your company.

extrovert

In the Myers-Briggs typology, an extrovert is a person who interacts easily with other people and has more interest in things outside the self than he does in internal thoughts and feelings.

Feeling

In the Myers-Briggs typology, people described as *feeling* are empathetic and subjective. They have a greater appreciation for the views of other team members, and they take an immediate view of the situation.

firewall

A firewall is a piece of software or hardware that keeps your network safe from intruders by screening them out.

Forming

In Bruce Tuckman's model of team development (1965), Forming is the first phase of development marked by little agreement on team aims and a high level of dependence on the team leader.

future state

In change management theory, the future state is the project's end point, when you assess your work, conduct the post mortem, disband the team, and move on to the next project. See also *current state; transition phase.*

given

The givens are facts or phenomena beyond your control that still hold sway over your project. For instance, a million-dollar budget may be a given, but a lack of time may be a given as well.

host

A host is a server (i.e., a large computer) that makes a website, database, or other shared resource available to users. A server is said to *host* a shared resource.

IGT rule

The IGT rule explains how teams evolve from individuals and groups, each with their own level of cohesion, teamwork, and common goals.

independent project review

See *IPR.*

Individuals Groups Teams

See *IGT rule.*

information meetings

Information meetings are designed to spread information, most often to your project team. These meetings are primarily used for daily updates and project updates. See also *action meetings; standup meetings.*

In The Rooms

See *ITRs.*

intranet

An intranet is a private website built and designed for the benefit of your project team. It cannot be accessed by people outside your firm and is most often hosted on servers your company owns and operates. Project intranets can include a huge array of features, from a library of project documents (such as the statement of scope, project charter, and so on) to online chat rooms or discussion forums.

Introvert

> In the Myers-Briggs typology, an introvert is a person focused on internal events, feelings, and emotions. Introverts often feel ill at ease in groups with other people; they may be perceived as shy or even timid.

intuition

> In the Myers-Briggs typology, intuition refers to the trait of people who prefer to gain understanding through insight, not hands-on experience. Intuitive types often think of the future and enjoy abstract, theoretical work.

IPR (independent project review)

> An IPR, as opposed to an audit, is an outside review of a project scheduled by the project manager herself, often at regular intervals for a project's duration. IPRs help the project manager and her team to see what they might have missed or find answers to problems they haven't solved. See also *audit*.

ITRs (In The Rooms)

> In a meeting, ITRs are people who sit in the room but not at the conference table. (They often sit in chairs by the walls.) ITRs tend to be junior staff or assistants, and as such, they're not expected to contribute to the meeting, as opposed to At the Tables (ATTs). See also *ATTs; OTPs*.

job cost report

> A job cost report details the costs of your project in line-item format. It also compares the projected cost of each item to its actual cost by adding its cost-to-date to its cost-to-complete. See also *cost-to-complete; cost-to-date; total cost; variance*.

Judgment

> In the Myers-Briggs typology, people with a preference for judgment (also called Judging) like a planned and orderly life. Control is important to them, and they like to keep things well-organized. They often plan their work in advance, to avoid rushing for deadlines.

Keirsey Temperament Sorter

The Keirsey Temperament Sorter is an alternative to the Myers-Briggs typology. It tests a person's temperament and assigns him to a category such as Inspector, Provider, Crafter, and so on. This test can help your team members learn about their personalities and communication styles, and, as such, it can help your team work better. See also *MBTI*; *MTR-i*.

Management Team Role-indicator (MTR-i)

See *MTR-i*.

MBTI (Myers-Briggs Type Indicator)

The Myers-Briggs Type Indicator (MBTI) is the granddaddy of personality tests. It's used in business and academe to assess a person's temperament and assign him or her to one of 16 categories marked by a combination of four letters: ESTJ, ESTP, INTJ, and so on. These types reflect how a person thinks and acts in groups; as such, these designations can help your team members understand how they react to others and communicate. See also *Keirsey Temperament Sorter*; *MTR-i*.

mediation

Mediation is a way of resolving disputes in which two parties who disagree meet with an impartial "judge" (called the mediator) and try to work out their problems. The mediator's job is to help the parties find compromise or common ground for their issues.

meeting facilitator

Also called the loudmouth, a facilitator is the person who runs a meeting. It's his job to keep the meeting on time and on track, to involve people who might be holding back, and to follow up after the meeting with activity items, minutes, and other reports.

memo to file

A special type of memo, the memo to file is sent from the project manager to the project sponsor or client at the start of a project. It confirms the joint commitment to the project. If the project sponsor or client should fail to perform his duties at some point, the memo to file is used to remind him.

mentor

A mentor is a person who acts as an advisor to someone of lower rank in his business. Mentors can be a valued source of help, advice, training, and even inspiration. See also *newbies*.

mind map

A mind map is a graphic technique for exploring a thought, concept, project, or plan. Invented by Tony Buzan in the 1960s, mind maps use the full range of cortical skills (image, word, number, color, rhythm, and so on) to record a concept in a design that resembles the human neuron.

MTR-i (Management Team Role-indicator)

Like the Keirsey Temperament Sorter and the Myers-Briggs typology, the MTR-i is used to assess a person's temperament and assign him to a category, but, unlike Keirsey and Myers-Briggs, the MTR-i tends to focus on a person's role within a team, and how that role adds to team value. See also *Keirsey Temperament Sorter; MBTI*.

Myers-Briggs Type Indicator

See *MBTI*.

newbies

Newbies are simply people who are new to a project or team. They're often paired with mentors at the start of a project to help them adjust and integrate. See also *mentors*.

Norming

Norming is the third and sometimes final phase in Bruce Tuckman's model of team development. It's marked by the beginnings of group agreement and clarity of purpose. Roles are well-defined and accepted, and major decisions are often made in well-run team meetings. Team unity in this phase is strong.

OJT (on-the-job training)

OJT is a kind of training that an employee receives while still on the job, as opposed to training received while at school or on sabbatical. Often, OJT is the best way to train a team member, because it's done where he works and done in context. It's also far less costly than sending a person to school, which removes him from the workplace and disrupts the team.

on-the-job training

See *OJT*.

Pareto's Law

Also known as the 80/20 rule, Pareto's Law states that a relatively small number of elements in a population will collectively account for a very large percentage of the overall measure of the population. This is a fancy way of saying that 20 percent of anything will account for 80 percent of the results.

PCM (project control manual)

The PCM is a book or binder where crucial project documents are stored. This includes the project charter, statement of scope, schedule, budget, and all status reports, change requests, action items, and the like. Also called *project library*.

PDF (Portable Document Format)

Short for Portable Document Format, a PDF file is a computer file invented by Adobe Systems (www.adobe.com) in the late 1990s. PDF files can be read by any platform—Mac, Windows, Linux, and so on—so long as the computer in question is equipped with Adobe's Acrobat Reader software, which is available for free on the Adobe website.

Perception

Also called Perceiving, this trait in the Myers-Briggs typology refers to people who prefer a spontaneous and flexible way of life. They like to adapt to the world, and they like to stay open to new and enriching experiences. Often casual, Perception types like to keep detailed plans to a bare minimum.

Performing

Performing is the fourth and final phase of Bruce Tuckman's model of team development (1965). The Performing stage is marked by a strong degree of team unity and autonomy. With little help from its leader, the team functions as one, and often over-achieves its goals.

personal information manager

See *PIM*.

PIM (personal information manager)

A PIM is a piece of software that stores your calendar, contacts, task lists, and often e-mail as well. Far and away the most common PIM is Microsoft Outlook (www.microsoft.com/outlook). The Palm desktop is a PIM used by the owners of Palm handheld computers.

Pleasure and Displeasure List

The Pleasure and Displeasure List is a simple list of items, results, and actions that will please or anger a project's stakeholders. For instance, the CEO will be pleased by sticking to schedule, and angered by a project that's over budget. Pleasure and Displeasure Lists are written at the start of a project and used as guides for what to aim for and what to avoid as the project is executed.

PO (purchase order)

A purchase order is a short form authorizing the purchase of goods from a vendor. Each PO has a unique number and lists the goods to be purchased, as well as their price. A PO is often used in place of a contract.

Portable Document Format

See *PDF*.

post mortem

A post mortem is an examination of a corpse to determine the cause of death. In project management, a post mortem meeting is conducted after a project concludes to determine what, if anything, went wrong, what can be improved, and what needs to be strengthened in subsequent projects.

project charter
A critical project document, the project charter states the need for the project and defines its products or results. Writing the project charter should be the first step in any organized project.

project control manual
See *PCM*.

project library
See *PCM*.

project scope
The scope is the extent of a project, i.e., its work, its goals, and its products. It is what the project entails. The project scope is set forth in the statement of scope and should only be altered in writing when agreed to by all parties involved, including the project manager and the project sponsor. One of the worst (yet most common) problems on any project is scope creep, namely, the subtle ways in which projects grow in size beyond their original scope. See also *scope creep*; *statement of scope*.

purchase order
See *PO*.

range estimates
A range estimate is one in which each line item is given a range in dollars and not an exact amount. Hence, in a range estimate, the budget for steel may be listed as $1,000,000 to $1,200,000, with a total range of $200,000. Range estimates take into account possible changes in market price, demand, and errors in estimates.

request for clarification
See *RFC*.

request for information

>   See *RFI*.

responsibilities matrix

>   A responsibilities matrix is a chart that lists each member of the project team and shows his or her responsibilities.

RFC (request for clarification)

>   An RFC is a form sent to a project sponsor or client when his input is needed on a certain aspect of the project, most often its scope. By forcing the sponsor or client to clarify his needs in writing, project managers have a permanent archive of project directives.

RFI (request for information)

>   An RFI is a short, standard form sent to the client or project sponsor requesting his input on some aspect of the project. It can be used to clarify scope or to document a client's needs, and thus avoid confusion.

risk management

>   Risk management is the process of planning for uncertain events that can impact your project. The goal of risk management is to reduce the risk of such events in case they happen.

rolling wave

>   When planning a project, some project managers plan every step and detail from start to finish. This can make for large and bulky plans. Using the rolling wave concept, project managers plan only those events in the near future (defined as one to two months) in detail. Each period, the plan is moved forward by a corresponding amount.

rules of the road

>   The rules of the road are rules used by a project team to run efficient and orderly meetings. They include such guidelines as "Never cut off a team member while speaking" and "Start and end all meetings on time, with no exceptions."

scope creep

Scope creep is one of the worst (yet most frequent) problems on any project. It refers to the subtle ways in which projects grow in size beyond their original scope. Project managers must be careful to control scope creep at all points on a project. See also *project scope*; *statement of scope*.

scribe

Scribes (also known as note-takers or minute-takers) are neutral parties in a meeting. They capture ideas and decisions on a whiteboard or flipchart or by taking notes to distribute later. Scribes prepare the meeting minutes, and they work up action items and send them out to the team.

self-assessment

A self-assessment is a process in which a person identifies his own goals, strengths, and failings as a member of the project team. Self-assessments are often done yearly and written and saved for reference.

Sensing

In the Myers-Briggs typology, Sensing types are immersed in the rich world of sensory experience. They tend to think of the present, not the future, and often have a good hold on the facts of any situation. In addition, they also have a good eye for detail.

shutdown/turnaround project

A shutdown/turnaround project is a project whose timeframe is very short, often measured in hours or days. Shutdown/turnaround projects must be carefully planned and often practiced well in advance of their execution.

skills assessment

Skills assessment is the process in which a project manager or team leader notes and measures the skills of each of his team members. It results in a skills matrix. See also *skills matrix*.

skills matrix

A skills matrix lists the skills of each team member and quantifies those skills as beginning, advanced, or expert. See also *skills assessment*.

SME (subject matter expert)

An SME is an expert in a special field of study such as law, finance, physics, and so on. SMEs are often hired as outside consultants to a project, and they charge an hourly rate.

standup meetings

A standup meeting is a brief meeting in which no one sits. They are largely informational. Most standup meetings are held at the beginning of the day as status meetings or daily kickoff meetings, but they can also be held at the end of the day to review what's happened or to set the plan for the following day.

statement of scope

The statement of scope is one of the most basic and crucial of all project documents. It lists, in some measure of detail, what the project entails and what it will deliver. The statement of scope should always be written at the start of a project and approved and signed by the project sponsor and project manager. See also *project scope*; *scope creep*.

stoplight chart

A stoplight chart is a simple chart named for its use of stoplight icons in the right-hand column. List your open tasks on the left-hand side of the chart, and on the right-hand side, assign an icon to each task: green for good, yellow for caution, red for alert. A stoplight chart is a good way to communicate problems to upper management, who are often too busy to read lengthy reports.

Storming

In the Forming, Storming, Norming, Performing paradigm designed by Bruce Tuckman (1965), Storming is the second phase of project team growth. In this phase, team unity is low as cliques and factions often form and challenge the team leader's control. At this stage, the team is still inefficient and suffers from internal squabbles.

storyboard

A storyboard is a graphic series of panels that depict each step in a project. It's often used for shutdown/turnaround projects where the project scope is highly defined and the project schedule is defined in hours or days.

stress points

Every project has its stress points—moments in time when the project team is put to the test and the project itself is jeopardized. Common stress points involve the loss of a team leader, a product rollout, and so on.

subject matter expert

See *SME*.

SWOT analysis

SWOT stands for strengths, weaknesses, opportunities, and threats. A SWOT analysis can be conducted at the start of a project as part of the risk management process.

task-switching

Task-switching is the act of switching from one task to another and starting to focus on the new task. In 2001, a University of Michigan study found that 20 to 40 percent of our productivity is used up in task-switching. This is strong evidence that multi-tasking is not the best way to work; in fact, it may waste time.

Thinking

In the Myers-Briggs typology, Thinking types are cool and objective. They're highly analytical and seek to determine the objective truth of any experience. They may have technical or scientific bents, and they rely on logic, not intuition, to solve problems.

threads

    A thread is a branch of a discussion in a web-based discussion group. A discussion often has several threads, one for each subtopic.

total cost

    In a job cost report, the total cost refers to the total cost of a line item, that is, the cost-to-date plus the cost-to-complete. See also *cost-to-complete; cost-to-date; job cost report.*

transition phase

    In change management theory, all projects have three segments: the current state, the transition phase, and the future state. The transition phase is where all the work gets done, that is, the actions that take the project from the current state to the future state.

variance

    In a job cost report, the variance refers to the amount by which the total cost of a line item differs from its projected cost. See also *job cost report; total cost.*

virtual team (VT)

    See *VT.*

VT (virtual team)

    A VT is one in which the team members are scattered across the state, the nation, or even the globe. VTs must rely on technology to communicate and finish a project. They often meet by phone, e-mail, online discussion, or web conference such as WebEx.

WBS (work breakdown structure)

    A work breakdown structure is simply a division of a project into all its extensive tasks and subtasks.

web browser

    A web browser is software that is used to surf the World Wide Web. The two most common web browsers are Internet Explorer and Netscape Navigator.

WebEx

WebEx (www.webex.com) is a website that provides online meetings to firms of any size. Using WebEx, you can share slides, memos, letters, spreadsheets, video, and more in real time, using nothing more than your web browser. See also *web browser*.

weekly status report

A weekly status report is a one-page report written each week by the project manager. It's a snapshot of the project's status, and it details what's been done in the last week, what must be done this week, any problems or issues that need attention, and any special resource requirements in the upcoming week.

work breakdown structure

See *WBS*.

Index

Note to the reader: Throughout this index **boldfaced** page numbers indicate primary discussions of a topic. *Italicized* page numbers indicate illustrations.